To Arthur B. Clar...

To our nephew whom
we have loved greatly throughout
his whole lifetime —
Uncle Leslie and Aunt Ardyce

W. Leslie DeLisa

in the world...

"It is incumbent upon the Saints . . . to so conduct themselves in the carrying into operation the details of their organizations as to be *in the world* but not of it, living and acting honestly and honorably before God and in the sight of all men, using the things of this world in the manner designed of God, that the places where they occupy may shine as Zion, the redeemed of the Lord."

—Doctrine and Covenants 128:8b, c.

in the world...

By G. Leslie DeLapp

Copyright © 1973

HERALD PUBLISHING HOUSE

Independence, Missouri

Library of Congress Catalog Card No. 73-75884
ISBN 0-8309-0099-3

Printed in the United States of America

This book is dedicated

TO MY WIFE, ARDYCE
AND OUR CHILDREN

Cicely Anne McGraw
Patricia Lucile Marsh
George Leslie DeLapp, Jr.

 CONTENTS

 **PREFACE**

In this biographical commentary G. Leslie DeLapp gives his readers glimpses into his personal life. He also bears his testimony about values which have developed over a lifetime rich in experience and service.

We do not wish to review in this preface the data about birth, baptism, ordinations, and assignments. In his introduction Bishop DeLapp shares some of this information and puts it in the context of his experiences as a whole. We are greatly impressed, however, with certain elements throughout the book which deserve to be noted with emphasis.

One of these elements is that of incarnational ministry. Repeatedly, our attention is drawn to the experience-centered interest which the author demonstrates in the Cause of Zion. "I have found," he writes, "that one cannot separate himself in the development of concepts from the *sum total of all experiences of life . . .*" (page 14). Again, he tells of a growing concern as a child "to participate in the building of a community where there could be freedom from want, elimination of poverty, where educational, cultural, and economic opportunities could be extended to all" (page 16). Pursuing the concept into other realms he testifies that he cannot help but feel that science and religion may work together to the unfolding of the divine purpose in the age in which we live (page 29) and that "our Zionic horizon challenges us to a merging of spiritual and temporal in the everyday activities of life. This merging of the spiritual and temporal constitutes the great purpose of the Restoration gospel" (page 32).

A second element deserving major attention is his testimony about the spirit of ecumenism in the sense in which it is particularly appropriate to the Cause of Zion. From almost the first page he gives credit to the universal ministries of the Holy Spirit as expressed through people and agencies in many times and places. There is no exclusivism in the spirit of this book. The author was able to say that from his earliest childhood his friends represented all sections of community and religious interests. This testimony continues through the passing years, and he expresses appreciation for those who have respect for their own religious affiliations and beliefs, even though they differ from his (page 15). He also says, "Great religions have contributed to man's thinking and to his experience. Each one bears some evidence of man's searching for and often experiencing God" (page 33). Such insights lead naturally to the conviction that "all religious and racial groups should have equality in relation to the rights which democracy provides for its citizens. Those who may feel that they are the 'chosen few' have no priority in God-given rights intended for all men" (page 102).

While resisting the idea of an organic union of all Christian denominations as one institution, the ecumenical spirit is expressed in his testimony, "I agree . . . that many churches have wonderful objectives and insofar as possible all churches should work together for the common good" (page 102).

That Bishop DeLapp is a patriotic man is evident throughout the book. His overview, however, is international and intercultural. Readers will sense that many of the illustrations which he draws from United States history and social development have significance for many other national and cultural situations. Those who do not have a background of life and citizenship in the United States are encouraged to be alert to the appropriate extension of principles to their circumstances, exploring their own national and cultural heritage for insights relative to such principles.

May the spirit of the epilogue move in those who read: "Service to the community is both a privilege and a responsibility." We are grateful that Bishop DeLapp has shared with us his testimony.

THE FIRST PRESIDENCY

INTRODUCTION

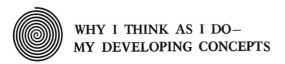

WHY I THINK AS I DO—
MY DEVELOPING CONCEPTS

In recent years some of my friends among the official personnel and throughout the local areas of the church have encouraged me to put in book form the thoughts and the experiences which have been mine in relation to the Cause of Zion. This encouragement has stimulated me to attempt such an undertaking, although I am quite aware of my own limitations in adequately expressing my thoughts, my deepest convictions, my hopes, my faith, and my desires in relation to the church to which I have given many years of service.

I believe it is worthwhile to approach this with some background information which may be helpful in presenting a point of view as well as developing an understanding of the work of the Bishopric. To do this, I am taking certain liberties in presenting material of a personal nature which might assist those who wonder why I think as I do and how my thinking has affected the policies and procedures in financial administration of the work of the church. Many people, ideas, and events have contributed to the development and administration of that policy; however, the Presiding Bishop and his counselors are held largely responsible for it.

My experience as Presiding Bishop covered a period of twenty-six years—1940 to 1966. Prior to this I served for nine years (1931-1940) as counselor to the then Presiding Bishop, L. F. P. Curry; three years as a stake bishop; and two years as bishop of Minnesota District.

I have found that one cannot separate himself in the development of concepts from the sum total of all experiences of life or from the friends and associates he has had from childhood. My view of the purpose and mission of the church had its beginning when I was five years old.

My father's people had been members of the original church. My mother was a convert—through my father's family—and her convictions of the divinity of this church never wavered throughout her life.

When I was two, my parents moved from East Delavan, Wisconsin, where I was born to White, South Dakota. After living in White for two years, we moved to Brookings, South Dakota, some fifteen miles distant. Some of the happiest days of my life were spent there.

In this community we made friends of various social and religious interests. Predominant among the active denominations were Baptists, Catholics, Christian Scientists, Episcopalians, Methodists, and Presbyterians. We happened to be the only members of the Reorganized Church. Occasionally we were invited to join other churches but we were never pressed to do so or in any way embarrassed. I attended a Presbyterian Sunday school and enjoyed my association with other youngsters. My teacher—Mrs. Wilson—had a keen interest in children and an appreciation of the religious preferences of others. From her I obtained a real sense of values to be found in religious groups.

Each year I was extended an invitation to become a member of the Presbyterian Church, and every time I discussed the matter with my parents, who in turn explained how the beliefs of that church differed from those of the one to which they belonged. I cannot recall that they made any adverse criticisms of other religious groups. Consequently, through the years I have learned to admire those who have respect for their beliefs, even though they differ from mine.

Other influences in the community also contributed to my thinking. It was quite common for the children of all denominations in the community to mingle. It was customary for the churches to hold their Christmas programs on different nights so that more people could attend. This probably was the beginning of my interest not only in our church but in community welfare and organization. We were welcome to participate in the activities of any church. All children shared in the good things that some of the more affluent families had—ponies, sleighs, and tennis courts. We had the privilege of fishing and swimming in the Sioux River or in a swimming hole in College Creek north of town.*

While I was a child, it was our privilege to have occasionally in our home missionaries of the Reorganized Church—men like Eli Hayer, Alvin Knisley, Edward Rannie, and Leonard Houghton. They would stay for days, and the discussions which took place as they visited with us often had to do with the subject of Zion. They emphasized the gathering of God's people, the second coming of Christ, and the purpose of evangelization; they also held out hope for the building of the kingdom. They stressed that life is of eternal character, but more than anything else they placed emphasis on the fact that man has agency—the right to think, to plan, to worship as he pleases. In their interpretation of law they

---

*When in Europe in 1947 with F. Henry Edwards of the First Presidency and M. A. McConley of the Council of Twelve, I met in Berlin a man who was in charge of religious affairs. He had lived in Brookings and he said that his boys had gone to that same swimming hole in the Sioux River by the railroad trestle. This contact, born out of similar experiences, was quite helpful to us while we were in Berlin.

stressed the importance of the individual's responsibility for service in the building of the kingdom. It was from these discussions that I began to get the concepts of a Zionic community. I wanted to participate in the building of such a community where there could be freedom from want, where educational, cultural, and economic opportunities could be extended to all. I found myself more and more interested in Zion and in other broad objectives of the church and decided to join it. This I did at the age of thirteen.

Even in that community—which, for the most part, was composed of professional, business, and laboring people—there were those who lived in proverty. My father received an average—or, perhaps, a little below average—income. From my very early boyhood I had to take advantage of every opportunity for employment to augment it. I worked as a Western Union messenger; I established a popcorn route; I worked as a water boy for a ditch-digging outfit; I weeded long rows of vegetables in a truck garden close to town; I pulled mustard from the fields of grain at the college farm; occasionally I had opportunity to caddy for a few of the wealthier citizens who played golf in one of the cow pastures north of town; I mowed lawns.

For recreation I would go out in the country to one of the creeks to watch the suckers run on a cold day, work on the one bicycle that we owned in the family, and make boomerangs from laths, bows and arrows from umbrella ribs. I belonged to a baseball team composed of youngsters ten to thirteen years of age. Uniforms were given to us by the sponsoring merchants, and we were sent to neighboring towns to compete with other boys' teams.

I remember my first ride in a Brush automobile. Its owner lived somewhere up near the college. Frequently it would get about as far as our place, which was in the middle of town, and then stop. It seemed always to be in need of repair.

Those were the days of great political campaigns. We boys were always eager to carry torches in the parade for any candidate. We had the privilege of marching once when Teddy Roosevelt was campaigning.

In looking back, I realize that one develops a code of ethics in the formative years of his life. Community life was different then, yet the development of an ethical concept through association, fellowship, and community endeavors was much the same as it is today.

In 1909 we moved to Minneapolis where there was a small congregation of our church. I was the only one of my age in the group, but I attended quite consistently, participating in the services as I had opportunity and taking part in other activities. We were, in a sense, "isolated," since our home was some distance from the church; so I often attended the Methodist Church a few blocks away.

I liked sports and soon made friends in North Minneapolis who played baseball, football, and hockey. It was not long until I was invited to become a member of the baseball team of the Methodist Church. This, too, was an excellent experience. I got acquainted with a number of fine boys, one of whom later became a pitcher for the Washington team. High school life was full of activity. In addition to my academic responsibilities I tried out for the track, hockey, and baseball teams and lettered in each of these sports. I was also elected business manager of the hockey team. Here again I found many things of common interest and learned something of the value of friendships with people of all faiths.

However, it seemed to me that the more I learned about our own church and others, the more fully I sensed the broader scope of the doctrine—and particularly the social philosophy—of the church of the Restoration. The ideals embodied in the commission to establish the Cause of Zion not only interested me but stimulated my thinking relative to the building of a community where people could function more efficiently as stewards, where poverty could be eliminated, and where the fullest opportunities for development could be provided. Throughout the years I have found increased interest in the attainment of these major objectives. At the same time I have noted the tremendous developments that have taken place (particularly within our own country) to improve the standard of living, and provide social and cultural benefits.

During my high school years I had to work in order to cover expenses at school and have spending money. One summer I buffed cans in a biscuit factory. Later I got a better job working at a truck farm for my board, room, and thirty-five dollars a month. After finishing high school I got a job in the Security National Bank in Minneapolis. I worked there and in the First National Bank (which absorbed it) for four years. At night I studied. I took the American Institute of Banking courses, university extension work, and learned as much as I could about the banking business.

In June 1917, during World War I, I enlisted in the Medical Corps. I served as quartermaster sergeant, mess sergeant of several field hospital companies, and eventually top sergeant of a field hospital company. I finally transferred from the Medical Corps at Camp Lewis, Washington, to the Cavalry Officers Training School at San Antonio, Texas. I had just two more weeks to go to get my commission when the armistice was signed and the school was discontinued. I received my discharge as sergeant first class in the Cavalry.

When I returned to Minneapolis to take up employment

with the bank where I had worked I found that many changes had taken place; in almost every department there was some person with many years of seniority. After six months I handed in my resignation. To my surprise, two of the officers suggested that I wait and see if they could find a better opening for me, which they did. I went into the office of Mr. F. A. Bean, the founder of International Milling Company, in Minneapolis. Mr. Bean was one of the finest men I had ever met. At that time he was eighty years old and not actively engaged in the administration of the company, which was headed up by his son. Over a period of years Mr. Bean had acquired some 40,000 acres of land in Canada, over 12,000 acres in California, and other properties in Minnesota and North Dakota. These holdings were being administered under the name of F. A. Bean Properties, Inc., and other subsidiary companies.

It was my privilege to work here for nine years. Both Mr. Bean and Mr. Crinkley, the secretary, were willing to teach me about the business—and business in general. Under them I received training in accounting, farm operation management, land purchase and sale, and practically everything pertaining to general business principles. I learned how to make financial statements, income and expense statements, consolidated balance sheets, income tax reports, et cetera. I acquired considerable knowledge that has been helpful to me in the work of the church. Not the least important was the training I got in business ethics under these men.

There are many things which have to be left unsaid, but the life of the pastor of the Minneapolis Branch was of such high character as to challenge me always. He had a favorite quotation from the scriptures:

And the Lord God spake unto Moses, saying, The heavens, they are many and they can not be numbered unto man, but they are numbered unto me, for they are mine; and as one earth shall pass away, and the heavens thereof, even so shall another come; and there is no end to my works, neither to my words; for this is my work and my glory, to bring to pass the immortality, and eternal life of man.—Doctrine and Covenants 22:23.

The fact that this was an expression of the Divine Mind came to me in no uncertain way as I contemplated it and the meaning of life eternal at the time of the death of my sister's little daughter. That expression came with such clearness while I was attending the funeral and for days afterward that I felt it absolutely vital that I devote my life, my efforts, my talent, my all to the work of Jesus Christ.

The background of such an experience was in part related to the fact that upon returning from military service in 1918 I had expected to be active in church. However, the congregation was in the throes of dissension, and I decided that religion was not for me. I quit attending church for a period of years. The death of my niece, however, caused me to do some reevaluation. After critical introspection and self-analysis I found I needed to reconstruct my thinking.

I soon became actively engaged in church work at both local and district levels. I was called to the priesthood—first as a priest, then as an elder, and in 1926 I was ordained a high priest and bishop.

In July that year I was married to Ardyce Lucile Case, the daughter of Seventy and Sister Hubert Case who had served the church since 1894, giving the first four years of their life together as missionaries in the Society Islands. In January 1928 our first child, Cicely Anne, was born. We had expected to make Minneapolis our home, but we were asked to accept General Church appointment to Lamoni, Iowa, where I was to serve as stake bishop.

With considerable hesitation—and only after prayerful

consideration—I decided to leave Mr. Bean. I accepted the appointment on March 1, 1928.

Throughout the years I have learned many things about the work of the church. I have learned that growth comes only as we apply ourselves to the tasks at hand. There are ministries which, if accepted by those who seek them, prove of immeasurable help. Such an experience was mine when, as a young man, I received my patriarchal blessing.

... and if you are thus diligent, being very faithful, there will come to you by the inspiration of his Spirit the necessary call to occupy in due time in the priesthood of God. And if, when that call shall come unto you, you show yourself a willing and an obedient servant, your mind shall be so completely quickened that you will become duly qualified, both by natural ability and the power and presence of God's Spirit, you will become an instrument in the church and kingdom of God unto doing a great good among his people—a polished shaft in God's hand as an instrument of true and divine service.

It has taken me many years to learn that the "shaft" of human personality becomes polished only as the result of experience, study, hard work, self-discipline, concern for others and their problems. A polished shaft in the service of God is an instrument that must be kept ever at work; the polishing process is never completed. Sometimes I have wondered whether the material being polished is of the quality to withstand the hardships and trials that have had to be undergone. I have often questioned my own ability and fortitude. Such experiences, however, have led me to recognize my dependency on God and my need for association with my fellowmen.

I have learned, too, that ordination merely gives to the one ordained the authority to "become." The act itself does not fully equip him to serve. I found that being a bishop called for indoctrination in social philosophy, training in the general sciences, the humanities, economics, and administration of business. It also required an understanding of the fundamentals of church faith, including the basic law of temporalities.

Throughout my life I have sensed a divinity that has caused me to search for something beyond the physical world. Belief in God is fundamental, and I have found the need to continually question my thinking about and my relationship to him. My concept has expanded as new experiences, new ideas, and new philosophies have come my way. The more I study, the more avenues of thought open up to me. The search for a deeper knowledge of God is an unending one.

As I give consideration to that which I plan to discuss in the pages of this book, I would like to state that the policies of the church can but emerge out of the experiences of the past and the economic foundations already established. Our heritage of belief, faith, determination, and emotional and intellectual appreciation of our religion has impact beyond our ability to measure. The extent of this impact may best be observed in our interpersonal relationships. These are the things that have caused me to serve, to seek to build the kingdom, and to suggest procedures for the implementation of the temporal law of the Restoration church by its people, individually and collectively.

Two passages of scripture serve as the premise upon which further discussion will be based. The first is a definition of Zion:

> And the Lord called his people Zion, because they were of one heart and one mind, and dwelt in righteousness; and there was no poor among them.—Doctrine and Covenants 36:2h, i.

The other is contained in a revelation given to the church by Joseph Smith III in April 1909:

> It is incumbent upon the Saints while reaping the benefits of these organizations to so conduct themselves in the carrying into operation the details of their organizations as to be in the world but not of it, living and acting honestly and honorably before God and in the sight of all men, using the things of this world in the manner designed of God, that the places where they occupy may shine as Zion, the redeemed of the Lord.—Doctrine and Covenants 128:8b, c.

There must be something of a challenge in the biblical phrase "three-score years and ten" which causes men to want to attain it and then, having done so, evaluate what has been accomplished. Having achieved that span plus seven years, I think of the achievements and wonder if they will have lasting meaning and significance.

I have therefore decided to put in writing some thoughts and goals which have guided me throughout the years. Inasmuch as my life was motivated by the church I am giving primary consideration to the concepts which have been developed in relation to it and to the rest of the world with which I have come in contact. The church gave me incentive to serve and called me to align myself with its purpose, yet to live in the world, associate with all men of goodwill, and join hands wherever possible to build a better church and a better community. Therefore, I have decided to title these thoughts, "In the World. . . ."

Today there is need for evaluating the church and its goals in the light of an expanding economy and changing world conditions. Thus, after more than forty-six years of serving as a bishop in the church, I find it necessary not only to make an appraisal of what has happened through those years but to try to think through the place of the church in our present world and evaluate its potential contribution.

While the standard of living has been raised throughout the United States and in other countries and some of the cultural and social goals of the Restoration have been partially realized through civic and governmental agencies, there is still need for an ever increasing number of people to commit themselves to the cause of building the kingdom of God.

Related to the principal objectives of the church are education, health and welfare, care of the poor, land purchase, financial administration, community planning, and the development of democratic processes. I hope that the treatment of these and other subjects in the following pages will be helpful in presenting the comprehensive social and economic goals of the church as I see them in relation to that which challenges the thinking of all.

I have summarized the basis of my belief in the following rather succinct postulates:

1. God, the Creator—of the universe, the world therein, and man—through Jesus Christ, his Son.

2. "The Holy Ghost, which beareth record of the Father, and of the Son, which Father, Son and Holy Ghost are one God, infinite and eternal, without end" (Doctrine and Covenants 17:5).

3. The immortality and eternal life of man.

4. The universality of the stewardship of man over talents, time, and resources.

5. The accountability of man to God and to his fellowmen in such stewardship.

6. The right of man to enjoy that portion of God's creation essential to his fullest development.

7. The right of inheritance in that which such stewardship requires and justifies.

8. The geographical gathering of those of like minds, ideals, and beliefs respecting social, cultural, and religious life within the limits of physical and economic conditions.

9. The religious-economic organization of individuals and groups to attain "the more abundant life."

10. The basic principle of the voluntary consecration of surplus to the advancement of individual, group, and society.

11. The organization and implementation of the storehouse through the process of surplus consecration.

12. The ultimate accomplishment of the divine purpose— the establishment of Zion.

13. The divine commission of the Restoration church to promulgate the gospel of Jesus Christ to all nations, kindreds, tongues, and people as the basis of individual salvation and the attainment of the universal brotherhood of man.

14. The free agency of man to choose for himself that in which he shall believe, and to use talents, time, and resources voluntarily to further such beliefs and purposes subject to the moral and constitutional laws established by the society and state of which he is a citizen.

Chapter 1

 ETERNAL THREADS

Scriptural and Conceptual Background

Some passages of scripture have had special meaning and import for me because of their forthright declaration of the majesty and power of God as Creator of all. Further, they bear evidence of his concern for man—whom he created not only in the spiritual realm but as a living personality in the physical world—with firm promise of the fulfillment and realization of his kingdom, both now and in the world to come.

And it came to pass, that the Lord spake unto Moses, saying, Behold, I reveal unto you concerning this heaven and this earth; write the words which I speak. I am the Beginning and the End; the Almighty God. By mine Only Begotten I created these things.—Genesis 1:1, 2 (Inspired Version).

And I, the Lord God, formed man from the dust of the ground, and breathed into his nostrils the breath of life; and man became a living soul; the first flesh upon the earth, the first man also.—Genesis 2:8 (Inspired Version).

For unto us a child is born, unto us a son is given; and the government shall be upon his shoulder; and his name shall be called Wonderful, Counselor, the mighty God, the everlasting Father, the Prince of Peace.—Isaiah 9:6 (see also Isaiah 2:1-4).

And Jesus went about all Galilee teaching in their synagogues, and preaching the gospel of the kingdom; and healing all manner of sickness, and all manner of diseases among the people which believed on his name.—Matthew 4:22 (Inspired Version).

The thief cometh not, but for to steal, and to kill, and to destroy; I am come that they might have life, and that they might have it more abundantly.—John 10:10.

These and other scriptures (e.g. Doctrine and Covenants 11:1, 22:23, 10:3, 101:2; Book of Mormon, Mormon 4:26) form the basis of my belief that God is; that he revealed himself in the life and ministry of Jesus Christ, his Son; that the Restoration church was founded on the premise of present-day revelation; that revelations received through Joseph Smith, Jr., the founder of the church, contained principles governing the organization of the church; that these principles had application to the conditions and needs of men of that generation; that revelatory processes continued to find expression through Joseph Smith III, president and prophet of the Reorganized Church of Jesus Christ of Latter Day Saints; and further, that basic revelations given in those generations are of contemporary value in this generation. I believe these will stand the test of scrutiny and examination in our rapidly changing world.

It is my feeling that there need be little if any conflict between the message of the Restoration church and science. I think that ideas expressed by others in such terms as "secular Christianity" or "involvement in the affairs of the world" should be examined in the light that revealed truth does not require a separation of belief in God and the divinity of Jesus Christ. Furthermore, I do not lose faith in my basic concepts relative to the establishment of Zion because of the tremendous changes which have taken place in our world since the coming forth of the Restoration.

On the contrary, I feel that my faith in God increases despite such things as the pressures under which we live—wars, burgeoning communities, exploding population, complex business, expanding educational and religious goals, and individual prestigious status. These are basic problems affecting our relationships. These require us to explore spiritual realms which may be helpful in finding real purpose in life. If there is one need paramount in our day it is that of determining purpose in life. This applies not only to men of religion but also to men of business and science.

The criticisms that proliferate from many sources regarding the lack of leadership, disaffection, and fallibility existing within and among religious denominations is not without foundation, but the same may be true in regard to some in the field of science—for example, when research raises questions as to the validity of theories of scientists of past generations. Men should be ever in search of truth, whether in the field of religion or science.

Scientists are diligently trying to discover the origin of man and the beginning of the universe. A few years ago Dr. John O'Keefe, noted biophysicist, was questioned relative to the program of placing an American on the moon. One of the questions raised was "Do you hope to get clues on the moon of the beginning of life on earth?" the answer: "Not of life on earth so much as the beginning of the universe itself—or the absence of any beginnings."[1]

Along with millions of others, I sat close to the television set the night of July 20-21, 1969, eagerly watching that most marvelous demonstration of genius, faith, and courage, as two men emerged from the space capsule and walked on the surface of the moon. For days I had been thinking of that passage of scripture which came through Joseph Smith (referred to as "the Olive Leaf . . . the Lord's message of peace to us").

He that ascended up on high, as also he descended below all things, in that he comprehended all things, that he might be in all and through all things, the light of truth, which truth shineth. This is the light of Christ.

As also he is in the sun, and the light of the sun, and the power thereof by which it was made.

As also he is in the moon, and is the light of the moon, and the power thereof by which it was made.

As also the light of the stars, and the power thereof by which they were made.

And the earth also, and the power thereof, even the earth upon which you stand.

And the light which now shineth, which giveth you light, is through him who enlighteneth your eyes, which is the same light that quickeneth your understandings which light proceedeth forth from the presence of God, to fill the immensity of space.

The light which is in all things; which giveth life to all things; which is the law by which all things are governed; even the power of God who sitteth upon his throne, who is in the bosom of eternity, who is in the midst of all things.—Doctrine and Covenants 85: 2b-3.

I cannot help feeling that present-day science and religion may work together in unfolding the divine purpose. Many periodicals carry articles dealing with the development of science in various fields. In an issue of *Time* magazine[2] the subject of archaeology is covered in such a way as to give some understanding of the tremendous scope of man's searching in this field. The facilities and equipment with which we are now provided make it possible to establish dates and other information more specifically than at any time in history. The finding of the Dead Sea Scrolls has shed new light upon the period immediately preceding the time of Christ. Newspaper feature stories, such as the one found in the *Kansas City Star* on Antarctica,[3] are of great interest.

Many more illustrations could be given that contribute to the fund of knowledge being accumulated which calls attention to the fact that man's interest goes beyond this present life, reaching into the background of history, exploring evidences of previous civilizations, and searching for the answers to questions which men long have had relative to their creation and development.

In 1832 a revelation to the Saints challenged them to achieve high purpose:

> Also, I give unto you a commandment, that ye shall continue in prayer and fasting from this time forth . . . that you shall teach one another the doctrine of the kingdom; teach ye diligently and my grace shall attend you, that you may be instructed more perfectly in theory, in principle, in doctrine, in the law of the gospel, in all things that pertain unto the kingdom of God, that is expedient for you to understand; of things both in heaven, and in earth, and under the earth; things which have been; things which are; things which must shortly come to pass; things which are at home; things which are abroad; the wars and the perplexities of the nations; and the judgments which are on the land; and a knowledge also of countries, and of kingdoms, that ye may be prepared in all things when I shall send you again, to magnify the calling whereunto I have called you, and the mission with which I have commissioned you.—Doctrine and Covenants 85:21.

History has been written, research conducted, books and tracts published, and information disseminated in an effort to evaluate the movement which emerged from the startling experience of the boy Joseph Smith. Some who wrote were scoffers; some were enemies who wanted to destroy that which they either did not understand or feared; others were adherents who sought to confirm the divinity of the Restoration movement. Those who believed the testimony of Joseph Smith often were subjected to scorn, doubt, suspicion, and persecution. For some it was a test of faith. Often it meant the giving of life itself. Many have had to weigh the revelations which came through Joseph Smith, evaluate them in the light of prophetic utterances of ancient days, and match them against the historic and sacred literature which bears testimony of Jesus Christ and of those who were close to him in his ministry among men.

We can understand and appreciate the Restoration only in small degree. However, even so we can see in it a continuation of the work of God based on scriptures of the past. Its place in history is made possible because of God's contact with men down through the centuries. Each great leader—from Abraham to Christ—looked toward the realization of the kingdom. As we review that which is available to us, we sense that expanding horizons have always been before those who have sought to find God.

In the physical sense, we think of the horizon as the line or circle around which earth and sky seem to meet. To an observer, the distance of the horizon varies according to the height from which he is observing. Thus, the higher his position the more distant the horizon becomes. An analogy may be drawn from this in respect to the kingdom. Our intellectual and spiritual insight will determine the distance to our Zionic horizons. The goals have been set forth in prophetic utterances of the Old Testament prophets, in the gospel message of Jesus Christ, and in the revelations given to the Restoration church. We accept and believe in the common goals of the Christian Church, but specifications for implementation are more clearly set forth in latter-day revelation.

The broad objective is the achievement of that condition referred to in Doctrine and Covenants 36:2h, i: "And the Lord called his people Zion, because they were of one heart and one mind, and dwelt in righteousness; and there was no poor among them."

Our nation has established many great goals which range from equality in health, welfare, and education for its citizens to the elimination of hunger in countries of the free world.[4] Overcoming poverty has become one of the foremost goals of our nation, but there are concurrent problems which relate to the development of skills and attitudes which will have to be resolved before any program can succeed. It is in this area that our church has much to contribute. I believe that the disciplines essential to the achievement of this condition are to be found in the principles of stewardship, consecration, agency, and accountability. Essential procedures and organizations to be effected are the gathering, the storehouse, and group stewardships, including the Order of Enoch. The visibility of these on our horizon depends upon the combination of certain essentials such as experience, cumulative knowledge, skill, attitude, devotion, and belief. These establish the height from which we view the horizon of Zionic goals and objectives.

This analogy may be carried further in that our Zionic horizon challenges us to a merging of spiritual and temporal in the everyday activities of life. This merging constitutes the great purpose of the Restoration.

Religious Thoughts in a Complex World

Despite all the problems and dilemmas we are most fortunate to be living today. We do not need to be confused or overwhelmed by the accumulation of literature which has to do with history and the movement of God among peoples. Quantity staggers the mind. If one were capable of learning even a small portion of what is available in the literature of history or the sciences or religion and could relate knowledge acquired to the present world he could undoubtedly find purpose and meaning beyond that which we have discovered thus far. However, it is for us to glean a little here and a little there and piece it together as best we can. But all too few have the will to acquire knowledge and the capacity to use it to further human welfare. To increase this number through the channels of our educational and religious structure is a tremendous challenge.

If it were not for the mass of evidence accumulated down through the centuries of man's search for and contact with God, it would seem presumptuous to state that eternal threads are visible to those who diligently apply mind and spirit in an attempt to see them. As I have sought to find answers to questions concerning my own being, I have at times been thrilled with the expectations of life both "in time and in eternity." I have also experienced the frustrations and disappointments arising out of my own limitations in trying to comprehend that which has been available to me in the way of literature as well as in personal experiences. Sometimes these experiences have been unexplainable but they nevertheless have borne testimony of the eternal quality of life.

In past centuries great religions have helped to shape man's thinking. Each bears some evidence of his searching for and often experiencing God. Dr. Paul Hutchinson, in an introductory chapter of *The World's Great Religions,* has stated:

> Such young and fascinating sciences as anthropology, archaeology and paleontology are constantly uncovering new evidence concerning the life of our paleolithic ancestors. The evidence brings to light infinite variations, but on one thing it agrees. Man is a religious being.
>
> However and wherever he developed, from the time he became man, man has worshipped, and has often shown a belief that he possesses an immortal soul. His irresistible urge to worship has been explained by a leading American anthropologist, William Howells, who says that man, unlike other animals, is "the creature who comprehends things he cannot see and believes things he cannot comprehend."[5]

A. Eustace Haydon, in his book *Biography of the Gods,* states:

In the bewilderment of this confusion of tongues the Christian God keeps a precarious hold upon the thought of the intellectuals. Meanwhile, Christianity as a living religion has been turning with serious purpose during the last three decades toward the solution of the social problems of human living. If this practical movement should gather into itself the trained workers capable of leading it to success, and the values for which the Christian God has stood—love, justice, peace, security, and consolation—can be realized in human relations, the layman will not be greatly troubled by the conflicting reports brought back by theologians and philosophers from their adventures into the unknown.[6]

Those of us who believe in the message of the Restoration are confronted with problems comparable to those of followers of other religions. We need to know the background history of the nations to which we expect to send missionaries. We need to know the taproots of our own church and its message. We need to reexamine the revelations of Joseph Smith in relation to church and world needs. We must also look to the recorded words of ancient prophets to understand and evaluate their message and the impact of that message on civilization. Likewise, we need to consider the great religions of the present.

There are many parallels to be found in Judaism and Christianity—particularly in the Restoration church. A leading Jewish spokesman, Dr. Mordecai M. Kaplan, defines Judaism as a civilization:

... and the Jews as a people linked by a common history, and a common language of prayer, a common and vast literature, and a sense of common destiny ... its real drama is its history, its greatest image an idea—the idea of the One Living God.[7]

The eyes of the world have been focused on Palestine in recent years. The finding of the Dead Sea Scrolls brought new interest in relating philosophies such as "all things common" (Acts 2:44; 4:32) and disciplines of the people who wrote them with the period and peoples of the time in

34

which Christ lived; they also point out the messianic content of the teachings of that period. Research is intensified; old manuscripts coming to the light of day give knowledge of people and customs identified more closely to the time of Christ.[8]

There has always been interest in the section of the world where Christianity originated. Herman Wouk in his book *This Is My God* tells of the people he met on his visit to Israel:

> They can nearly kill you with kindness, hospitality, and demonstrative pride. You must see the potash works, and the cement factories, and the auto assembly lines, and the hospitals, and the farm communes, and the sulphur mines, and the yeshivas, and the technical schools, and the children's villages.[9]

Today thousands of Jewish people are seeking to regain Israel, the land of their inheritance. This movement took on momentum following World War II. In those first years living conditions were deplorable but, with determined convictions as to their rights and with hope for their future, they established themselves. Surely this denotes motivation beyond that of a migratory nation seeking only a place to live. It suggests the presence of an inner drive born of a conviction of divine purpose.[10]

Renewal of such interest is evidenced by Kenneth Machaish[11] in a description of the trip he made in an attempt to follow the travels of Abraham from Ur near the mouth of the Euphrates up to Haran, on to Beersheba, and over into the Land of Goshen, which is in the Valley of the Nile. He helps his readers visualize the conditions under which Abraham lived (many of which continue today). He describes his visit to the cave believed to contain the bones of Abraham, Isaac, Rebekah, Jacob, and Leah and tells how the shrine has been protected down through the centuries. As to its authenticity, he states:

But one may believe that the mortal remains of the patriarchs are there. . . . Perhaps it doesn't matter. The darkness beneath the brass bars in the floor of the mosque is enough. The burial cave is below. Here the weary wanderer was laid to rest in the only bit of land he ever owned. Here the long voyage ended. And here we latter-day followers of the half-hidden trail from Ur to Egypt felt sure, for the first time, that our paths and Abraham's had met.[12]

I find encouragement in the fact that there have been times down through the ages when men have been able to reach beyond the present and envision eternal threads which lead upward. If these threads are not totally visible the full distance to heaven they are nevertheless guidelines to spiritual heights which beckon men onward and upward toward their destiny with God.

In my own experience, in periods of meditation, I have felt a touch of the divine in unexplainable ways which have brought assurance of the continuity of life. Because of this I view historical records and monuments of ancient civilizations with more than casual interest. I look for and find many evidences in our world of the consistency with which men have sought for an understanding of God. This search has been marked by periods of enlightenment in which they have been able to develop new concepts of their relationship to one another and to see more clearly their responsibility to God. There have been other times when it seemed that selfishness, war, and unbelief cast dark shadows over that light which men had previously received. Human characteristics have sometimes excluded the divine light. Successively, that light has broken through to help them see new paths which lead to progress toward God individually and through social organization.

Much has been found in antiquity which bears mute testimony of man's migratory but often lethargic past. Continued studies in the field of archaeology are revealing and will continue to reveal much that hitherto has been unknown about that past. People have searched for new lands, developed new countries, and then reverted to the old order of things. They have also been under the dominance of dictators as well as religious leaders who have exploited their followers to better maintain their own possession of economic and spiritual leadership. It is not at all surprising that many who read the records of these civilizations ask, To what end? For what purpose?

The scriptures reveal consistency on the part of God and his dealings with mankind which point always toward the culmination of his work. We need to know more about the origin of the scriptures that we might understand their contribution to those seeking to comprehend human development down through the ages and the underlying reasons for the laws given.

> The Bible came into being because of a movement that was taking place in the lives of men over a long period of time. The movement was essentially religious. God was involved in it to an extent in which, judged by any available evidence, he was involved in no other movement elsewhere. The movement slowly brought to light great truths about human life, which were always held to be inseparably connected with great truths about God, so much so that neither body of truths could long continue without the other, which is but to say that the Bible has finally but one theme—*God and his purpose with men.*[13]

Whether the scriptures and historical records have their origin in fact, tradition, imagination, or a combination of these, they are an expression of the divine urge men have to relate to their Creator. Without these guidelines we could be overwhelmed, if not lost, because of the limitlessness of space which science continually reveals to us. The scriptures provide stabilizing knowledge through the sacred historical record of God's revelation to man as found in the Old and

New Testaments. These have withstood the scrutiny, scoffing, and criticism of agnostics throughout the centuries.

Often in a period of contemplation, as I have scanned the heavens at night, I have been amazed and humbled because of the immensity of that which was visible to me, knowing that it was only a small part of God's great creation. Perhaps I have something in common with the renowned scientist, astronomer, and philosopher, Dr. Harlow Shapely, who stated:

> For centuries man has looked to the sky and wondered, "In this universe of stars, space, and time, am I alone?" After half a century of studying the heavens, I am struck by the inescapable conclusion that there *is* life in outer space; there must be. The laws of science leave me no other rational belief. [14]

The Wonder of Travel

I have been humbled as I have flown from country to country and witnessed the technological development being made. At such times I have felt that the intelligence of man is but a reflection of the intelligence of God. Trying to tie this all together causes me to have a greater desire to know more of history and more of God.

I thought of this a few years ago as I stood by the Nile River in a spot close to the city of Cairo where my Egyptian guide pointed toward the bank of the river and said, "Tradition has it that this is the spot where Pharaoh's daughter found the baby Moses." Tradition may not always be accurate, but the scriptures confirm that Moses was an important personality in bringing a great people to an understanding of God. Therefore, how can I help seeing God's hand in the life and leadership of Moses?

My thinking was stimulated again as I saw the contrasts between old Cairo and modern Cairo. In the shadow of modern dwellings people live in adobe huts as they did centuries ago. Carts drawn by donkeys wend their way amidst the congested traffic of automobiles on paved streets. Despite the evidence of civilization, I felt that the people of Egypt were more interested in the traditions of the past than the technology of today.

While there, I thought of the tremendous effect the completion of the Aswan Dam could have on the economy. At the same time, I felt that unless such a program aroused incentive for the Egyptians to qualify themselves physically, mentally, morally, and spiritually, the main purpose of the venture would be defeated. I thought of the tremendous task of our church in the field of stewardship directed toward the development of attitudes, skills, techniques, and knowledge, for these are acquired only by those who are willing to work and sacrifice for their attainment.

One cannot help deploring war and all its catastrophic consequences but one may also see therein the resultant intercourse of nations which imposes new thoughts, new philosophies, new customs, and in some instances even new hope for millions of people. Surely the hand of God reaches toward man constantly pointing the way toward higher goals.

As I viewed the pyramids and the Sphinx I thought of centuries past, as I presume every religiously inclined person must when he sees them. Their construction was motivated by some urge to project man's life into the future, but the builders obviously did not properly evaluate the worth of the human soul, for the construction was done by slave labor at a great cost of human life.

The Thread Holds

The eternal thread of contact between man and God continued as Moses transferred the leadership of the people to Joshua. The beginning of the national life of the Chosen People of God took place as they were about to enter into the land which had been promised to them: "Behold, I have taught you statutes and judgments, even as the Lord my God commanded me, that ye should do so in the land whither ye go to possess it" (Deuteronomy 4:5).

True to the promises which had been given, these people were permitted to see the waters of the Jordan divided and the city of Jericho taken. Subsequent years saw them gaining in power as they began a national life, overcoming some thirty-one kingdoms and dethroning their kings. The records bear substantial evidence that they were blessed when they complied with the law and that they suffered when they failed to comply with it.

The coming of Christ had been foretold through the prophets. Isaiah prophesied of the New World and the coming forth of the divine Word:

Woe to the land shadowing with wings, which is beyond the rivers of Ethiopia.—18:1.
And she shall be brought down, and shall speak out of the ground, and her speech shall be low out of the dust; and her voice shall be as of one that hath a familiar spirit, out of the ground, and her speech shall whisper out of the dust.—29:4 (Inspired Version).

This prophecy of Isaiah points up the divinity of the Book of Mormon. Specific application is found in Isaiah 29:11 (King James):

And the vision of all is become unto you as the words of a book that is sealed, which men deliver to one that is learned, saying, Read this, I pray thee: and he saith, I cannot; for it is sealed.

The Book of Mormon should be judged, however, not by biblical proof but by that which is found in its message.

The Book of Mormon is a story of an endeavor that did not work out all the time as God would have had it. There were times of spiritual heights and there were times of human degradation. The Book of Mormon brings in the human factor very forcefully. It affirms the

40

postulate of modern science that all things exist in relationships. It makes this inclusive; it says that God and God's universe have to be included in these relationships. It says that all humanity has to be included in these relationships. The Book of Mormon does not say that everything that happens is of God's designing. It calls men to catch hold of what God's design is for making history turn out his way.[15]

A More Complete Law of Christ

The coming of Christ began the greatest of all epochs in God's revelation of himself, particularly in the pronouncement, "Think not that I am come to destroy the law or the prophets . . . but to fulfill" (Matthew 5:19).

Jesus built upon the law which had been revealed through Moses and the prophets, elaborating the basic principles which govern moral and social conduct. He expanded it to embrace not only the Jewish people of that day but all men of all ages.

He gathered his disciples around him and taught them, and they believed in him "for he taught them as one having authority from God, and not as having authority from the Scribes" (Matthew 7:37). One of his disciples, Stephen, bore testimony of divine revelation even as he was being stoned, for he declared: "Behold, I see the heavens opened and the Son of Man standing on the right hand of God" (Acts 7:56) and evidenced the power of the gospel functioning in his life by saying, "Lay not this sin to their charge" (Acts 7:60).

It was no coincidence that Saul of Tarsus was standing by when Stephen made his petition to God, "and the witnesses laid down their clothes at a young man's feet, whose name was Saul" (Acts 7:58). It was the law of universal brotherhood to which Paul gave adherence following his experience on the way to Damascus when in vision he recognized Jesus as the Son of God. He later bore testimony as to his belief that obedience to the law bore fruit not only in the present

41

but in eternity as well: "But now being made free from sin, and become servants to God, ye have your fruit unto holiness, and the end everlasting life" (Romans 6:22).

Jesus presented certain fundamentals and principles to govern all aspects of life. He dealt with divorce, wealth, and covetousness not because they in themselves were evil but because of the effect they had on people.

The conditions under which Jesus lived were similar in many ways to those of today: autocracy in government, racial prejudice, internal dissension among the Jewish people, and oppression from without. Because of his knowledge of the composite nature of man he could always penetrate the depths of the human mind and soul as he did when he said to Zaccheus, "This day is salvation come to this house" (Luke 19:9). Illustrations such as this show the importance of attitude toward material possessions.

Through prophecies and in the life and ministry of Jesus, eternal principles have been revealed. They stand out in bold relief against the background of history to bring light and hope to a world that otherwise seems doomed. It is for each uf us to glean from them that which forms the basis of our personal philosophy.

While there are many passages of scripture from which selections can be made to form such a philosophy, I have found it necessary to study and evaluate each in relation to others. In the Restoration scriptures I find principles which are most helpful in developing an understanding of the means whereby temporal resources can be sublimated for the purpose of building Zion. These scriptures supplement and clarify the principles delineated in the Bible.

While there is considerable controversy over the details of the organization of the Church of Christ, both biblical and secular history confirm the tremendous impact made by

Jesus on the world of his day, as well as the centuries following. Early Christian history was marked by a spirit of unity that bound its adherents together. The more they were persecuted, the stronger the ties that bound them together. The editors of Horizon's *History of Christianity* express it in the following:

Early in Christian history the spirit of unity that bound the faithful ever more firmly together in the face of skepticism, ridicule, and persecution found expression in an organized polity that was to endow the Church with an enduring stability. It was this system of ecclesiastical organization that, combined with the principle of strong social authority, made the Church the most effective single factor in re-establishing the community of Europe after it had been shattered by the fall of Rome and the successive waves of barbarian invasions. During those critical years Christianity became, as it was to remain, the fundamental, cohesive force in the evolution of western civilization. Time and again over the centuries that were to follow, the indifference of the Church to worldly considerations, its stress upon purely spiritual concerns, made it a rallying point for the forces of life when temporal authorities could not stem the decadence of society.

Since the death of Christ his followers have known vicissitude as well as glory and authority. The Christian religion has suffered periods of persecution and critical divisions within its own ranks. . . . We live in what some have called the post-Christian age. Yet, wherever we turn to enrich our lives, we continue to encounter the lasting historical realities of Christian experience and tradition.[16]

The early Christian fathers did much to strengthen the church and helped to develop a "reverence for man." This is summarized by Robert Payne in his book, *The Fathers of the Western World*. Men like Tertullian, Ambrose, Jerome, and Augustine made specific contributions, and Christianity as a movement contributed to man's understanding of God. The Renaissance and the Reformation resulted in the development of broader concepts relative to God and Jesus Christ. Broader horizons were constantly developed which led men on to greater achievements.

My Personal Relationship to the Church

As I review history and find evidence of man's search for God, it does not seem strange to me that Joseph Smith, Jr., should have received divine revelations. From my own experiences I have found the need for some more clearly defined process by which man is to achieve God-given goals. The principles as taught by Christ need to be expressed in the lives of individuals through association in the corporate body of the church and in the community. An elaboration of these principles is found not only in the New Testament but also in the Book of Mormon, and their practical implementation is concisely set forth in the revelations given to the church through Joseph Smith III (such as in Sections 128 and 129 of Doctrine and Covenants). To me this is but additional evidence of God's desire and intent to accomplish his purpose—the establishing of his kingdom on earth.

The Base Has Been Formed

It is true that men's accomplishments thus far have fallen short of fulfillment of what God would have them achieve, but just as God is eternal, so is his purpose eternal, and through Christ there is hope of eternal life. We therefore approach the task of building his kingdom as a task not only for the present but also for eternity, since the thread of eternal progress extends through all dispensations of time. I believe it is expressed in the visitation of the angel to Joseph Smith which brought divine light to bear on man's responsibility to God through the restoration of the Church of Jesus Christ.[17]

The revelations which came to the church supplemented that which had previously been revealed in the scriptures and broadened the concept of a complete, full life. The Industrial Age brought new problems in human relations, and there was need for reiteration of the gospel law and its application to

44

meet present-day social needs. The revelations reemphasized the necessity for a new moral concept wherein God was recognized as Owner and man as steward.

The prophetic statement of the coming forth of "a marvelous work" brought hope to those who were seeking light and truth in that day of religious unrest, social and economic change which characterized the 1830s:

A great and marvelous work is about to come forth unto the children of men. . . . Now, as you have asked, behold, I say unto you, Keep my commandments, and seek to bring forth and establish the cause of Zion: seek not for riches but for wisdom; and, behold, the mysteries of God shall be unfolded unto you, and then shall you be made rich.—Doctrine and Covenants 6:1a, 3. (See also 3:15e, 16a; 5:3d; 6:3, 4; 12:5.)

Latter-day scripture tells of the coming forth of the divine plan respecting the temporal creation. Doctrine and Covenants 28, given in September 1830, contains a promise of the gathering and the coming of the millennium. There is also the statement that "all things . . . are spiritual" (paragraph 9) and that the use of temporal things is for the purpose of spiritual growth.

It is important, therefore, that we sense our place in the progress of God's eternal purposes. We could easily lose ourselves in the mass of individual and group conflicts, but we know that God has spoken through the ages, pointing the way, never losing hold of that thread of contact with man. And for that thread we, too, must reach, as men will ever reach eternally. When we make contact, new light, inspiration, and understanding lifts us upward. It is upon such premises that we seek to establish his kingdom here on earth.

One may well wonder what might have happened had those who were responsible for the Restoration movement in its inception remained true to the fundamentals upon which the church was founded. Specifically, revelation was basic, and from the very beginning Christ was the center of the new religious philosophy which made up the beliefs and doctrine of the Restoration movement. The secular aspects of it—such as the consideration which was given to the social ideals and objectives of the movement—were in a sense the disciplines by which those who believed in Jesus Christ as the Savior could build a life conditioned on the needs of the material world in which the Restoration, in a sense, intruded. The disciplines of stewardship, agency, inheritance, and the storehouse provided avenues through which men could adjust to this new age. These may be considered the ABC's of social amelioration.

Today, one is impressed with the development and implementation of social reforms which have been instituted by the government; these have resulted in materially fulfilling some of the objectives and goals of the Restoration. There is no question in my mind that the social ideals of the church have made impact on the thinking of others and contributed to the development of such social legislation.

There is need for further development of a program by the church to make clear the relationship of revelations dealing with the use of material possessions to the attainment of a new world order and also of the development of the Spirit to give evidence of the impact of Christ's teachings.

In doing this, we must draw upon the traditions, the scriptural authority, and the history of preceding centuries. It is my feeling that the Restoration came at a time when solutions were being sought for the problems which had arisen during the Industrial Revolution and guidance was needed for the advent of the age of scientific and technological development which followed.

1. *United States News and World Report,* August 20, 1962.
2. *Time,* December 13, 1963.
3. "Antarctica," *Kansas City Star,* January 29, 1967.
4. *Goals for Americans—The Report of the President's Commission on National Goals,* a Spectrum Book, Prentice Hall, Inc.
5. Dr. Paul Hutchinson, *The World's Great Religions,* page 1 of the introduction.
6. A. Eustace Haydon, *Biography of the Gods,* Macmillan Co., New York, 1944, pages 282, 283.
7. *Op. cit.,* page 133.
8. Millar Burrows, *The Dead Sea Scrolls,* Chapter 11; Dimont, *The Jews, God, and History;* James A. Michener, *The Source;* Leon Uris, *Exodus.*
9. Herman Wouk, *This Is My God,* pages 214-218.
10. Murray Winegarten, *Life in a Kibbutz.*
11. Kenneth Machaish, "Abraham, the Friend of God," *National Geographic,* December 1966.
12. *Ibid.*
13. Edwin Lewis, *A Philosophy of the Christian Revelation,* Harper and Brothers, Publishers, page 32.
14. Harlow Shapely, "The Riddle of God, Man, and Space," *Coronet* Magazine, February 1961.
15. Roy A. Cheville, *The Book of Mormon Speaks for Itself,* Herald House, 1971, pages 43, 44.
16. Horizon's *History of Christianity* (American Heritage), page 7.
17. *Church History,* Volume 1; Doctrine and Covenants 26:2; 110:20.

Chapter 2

THE CONTEMPORARY CHARTER
OF RESTORATION CONCEPTS

The Restoration church was founded in a period which was favorable to the introduction of a new philosophy of human relationships—new in the sense that it was more comprehensive in regard to the use of resources, talents, and time for the improvement and uplift of society as a whole. It also recognized a present-tense God—one who revealed himself in a time of religious unrest and sectarian doctrinal differences. In a sense, it was Utopian, having within it the best of Christian philosophy which had motivated other similar movements, yet lacking the restrictive and questionable communal relationships which had proved detrimental to some of them.

Looking back, one can see how the Restoration church could have served to a much greater degree had it remained steadfast to the commission given it through the revelatory process.[1]

It is difficult to properly evaluate all of the factors which had bearing on its beginning. Historians give scant coverage to its origin and impact on the religious and social life of the people of the early 1830s. However, throughout the years since its founding, the Latter Day Saint movement has come to be an important part of American history, particularly in the development of the West. Beginning in Palmyra, New York, its followers developed settlements at Kirtland, Ohio; Independence, Missouri; and Nauvoo, Illinois. Later, a large portion of the Saints went to Salt Lake, Utah. Then began a regathering of many who remained in the midwest, and by action of a conference at Amboy, Illinois, the church was reorganized under the leadership of Joseph Smith III. Subsequent settlements were at Plano, Illinois; Lamoni, Iowa; and finally Independence, Missouri. Other smaller groups dispersed to various areas including Wisconsin, Minnesota, Michigan, Pennsylvania, and Texas. (See *Story of the Church,* by Inez Smith Davis, chapters XXXVII-XLVI; Volume 3, chapters 7-9, *History of Reorganized Church of Jesus Christ of Latter Day Saints.*)

Before evaluating the relationship of the Latter Day Saint movement to the rapidly changing society of that time I reviewed conditions which existed prior to it.

There are two periods preceding the "coming forth" of the Restoration which are of primary interest to me—the Industrial Revolution and the "Period of Enlightenment" of the eighteenth century. Up to this time there were writers and philosophers whose names are familiar to all—Socrates, Plato, and Aristotle, for example. Nor do scientists underestimate the early discoveries and inventions such as those listed by Mumford in his book, *The Myth of the Machine,* which recounts the building of the pyramids. He points out how discoveries and inventions emerge from the application of human ingenuity to the needs of the time.

What took place in the minds of the philosophers of the eighteenth century not only contributed to the progress of the age but stimulated creative thinking in many fields, particularly in theology and social welfare. Here, as well as in science, there had been forerunners. The need for a period of enlightenment was evidenced in many social and religious aberrations of the Middle Ages as men reached out to explore, conquer, and enslave the people of other nations. "Christian missionaries sought to convert the heathen by fire and sword, if need be, to the gospel of peace, brotherhood, and heavenly beatitude."[2] There were, of course, men of good morals and high standards, too.

It was the aim of the philosophers of the eighteenth century enlightenment to discover a better way of life for man, new respect for nature, and the relationship of all the physical creation. The search for ore and oil also brought evidences of prehistoric life. Bones and relics that were uncovered took on new meaning; they made man feel a part of the past as well as the present, and turned his mind toward his future as a human soul.

Thus, too, an interest in the new Utopias developed. Some of these preceded the eighteenth century. The most widely known account is by Thomas More, written in the latter part of the fifteenth century. He gives a description of the ideal society as he conceived it, discussing labor, the selfishness of the rich, and the deprivations of the poor, all in respect to the value of human life in relation to the value of goods.

Among later philosophers were those such as Diderot and Rousseau who believed in the natural goodness of men. Rousseau particularly felt that society was to blame for human deterioration. He thought society and its institutions perverted man and forced him in opposition to his better self. Rousseau made an impact upon his generation that was unlike that of some of his contemporaries:

We shall picture him in three settings: (1) as a moralist who attacked the notion that progress results from advances in science and technology; (2) as an "outsider" who furthered the romantic sensibility and opposed it to the dominant nationalism; and (3) as the revolutionary thinker who first inscribed on the political banners of modern times the opposing slogans both of democratic and of totalitarian government.

Rousseau's new set of ideas—for they were all related unless worked into the rational system of society—threatened to blow it up. Thus, the second half of the eighteenth century was the scene of a precarious attempt by Western man to reconcile reason and emotions, science and morality, and to create for himself a society in which he could build the balanced life.[3]

Carl L. Becker in his book, *The Heavenly City of the Eighteenth Century,* takes the position that history had gradually replaced theology and that science had replaced philosophy.

The vision of man and his world as a neat and efficient machine designed by an intelligent author of the universe gradually faded away. Professors of science ceased to speak with any assurance of the laws of nature, but were content to pursue without any plan or design the business of observing and experimenting with something which is the stuff of the universe.[4]

It is not surprising that further adventures in the formation and development of community endeavors and societies should take place preceding the 1830s. As with other social movements, the Utopian idea may be said to be the product of writers and philosophers, implemented either by them or community leaders with some concept of human needs. The number of those organized is estimated to have been somewhere between thirty-five and forty. Included were such movements as the Oneida Community, founded in 1834 by J. H. Noyes, out of which evolved Oneida, Ltd., of Sherrill, New York.[5]

Robert Owens developed the New Harmony Society in 1825. This and others were popular for a period of time and included among their members some of the important writers of that time. (Nathaniel Hawthorne, 1804-1864, and Ralph Waldo Emerson, 1830-1882, were members.) The Brook

Farm community was organized in 1841 near West Roxbury, Massachusetts. This experiment originated under the leadership of George Ripley and his wife. They and a few stockholders formed an association and purchased two hundred acres. Their ideal was to live by the principles of cooperation. While it attracted the attention of noted people, it lasted only until 1847.

Robert Owens was much more successful. He was attracted to America because of its resources and opportunities. There were vast areas of land available; different groups of people had formed many communities; the government imposed few restrictions. In 1822 a New York society for promoting communities publicized extracts from the *New View of Society,* a book written by Owens and published in 1813. He had also been manager of the New Lanark Mills in England. Subsequently (1829) he gave this up and devoted his entire time and his fortune to furthering his socialistic ideas. He had many suggestions for social organization and reform, some of which were quite extreme; for example, the following:

His favorite plan was to remove children from their homes at the age of two, and to put them in government boarding houses which would provide equality in dress, food, education, and opportunity, thus producing real democracy.[6]

One of his projects was at New Harmony, Indiana (1824 to 1828); this failed, at a loss to him of some $200,000.

The development which took place in those years preceding the 1830s brought great social changes. Much of the thinking of the philosophers, scientists, and writers, as well as the businessmen and entrepreneurs of the period, was being implemented—new factories were being built; the conditions of labor and laborers were being scrutinized and studied; experiments were taking place. Population increased, transportation problems arose; religious life became more intense; areas in the west were settled and the resources of land and forest exploited without regard to the future of the nation. A multiplicity of factors influenced the social life of the people, and change in the economy was great; the effects were both good and bad. Consideration of some of these is essential in the evaluation of the Restoration church and its founding.

Religion

The development of the machine greatly affected the economy and life patterns. Simple agrarian living was replaced by an industrial society which seemed to have little concern for human welfare except in the few instances where men recognized their responsibility to their employees in providing good working conditions.

Religion was indeed a force in the development of people, controversial though it was. It was pursued by many as a way to salvation, but not particularly as a factor in social uplift.

The change taking place raised questions by all groups in the rapidly growing population—questions having to do with religious beliefs and philosophies and the pragmatism of the technological, scientific, and business segments of the new society. There were questions about theology, social rights, slavery, and politics. Liberalism and the piety of those who established the country because of the need for religious freedom were, in a sense, in conflict. Those who were not satisfied with the restrictive concepts of most of the religious groups sought to establish a movement which would enable them to find expression for what they conceived to be a better way. One such movement, called Transcendentalism, had among its followers Ralph Waldo Emerson and the

Reverend George Ripley, founder of the Brook Farm Community.

> To the ever-occurring enigmatic question of what a man must do to be saved, Emerson found no easy answer in expansion and material progress. Rooted in a section of the country with more than two hundred years of history, formed by German Romantics, the sacred books of the East, Plato and the Neo-Platonists, finding even the mild yoke of Unitarianism too restraining, Emerson created his answer in Transcendentalism, the creed that he himself expounded in his lectures as the idealism of 1842. Mankind he divided into materialists and idealists.[7]

Liberal thinkers had preceded Emerson and his group. Thomas Paine had made what was considered an attack on religion in his *Age of Reason.* However, he took the position that he was merely trying "to show a higher form of religion."

It is impossible to cover all the history of America and its relation to religious groups that came into being following the landing of the Pilgrims in 1620. The first President, George Washington, took office in 1789, forty-one years before the founding of the Restoration church. There had been only ten presidents (one of whom served but a month) up to the time of the death of Joseph Smith, Jr., in 1844. During that period scientific and technological progress was being made, and the nation was growing rapidly.

There was much missionary zeal, but the diversity of beliefs was confusing. Protestantism was predominant. Reform movements were numerous. "Christians emphatically considered themselves their brothers' keepers, with the sacred duty to convert those less knowing than themselves to proper ideas of piety and morality."[8] The new democracy of the United States was considered "the final and perfect government—God had taken a direct hand in human affairs to create a model for the rest of the world to follow."[9]

Robert Riegel in his book, *Young America,* refers to the decade from 1830 to 1840 as the "changing world." He comments on the religious emphases and sects of those days and includes a comment on Joseph Smith:

> Most intriguing of the new sects was the Mormon, led by Joseph Smith, Jr., but it was only symptomatic—Alexander Campbell had tried to persuade Christians to unite in a simpler and "purer" set of doctrines, but by the 1830's there was no question that what he had produced was one more sect.[10]

Tract societies were numerous and prolific in printing and distributing literature. The common folk of the 1830's and the preceding years felt the need for a personal God who was attainable beyond mind and reason alone. These might well have been called the fundamentalists. The intellectuals or liberals of the period were turning to Unitarianism and comparable philosophies, and the masses were responding to the evangelism of other sects, particularly the Baptists and the Methodists. Itinerant preachers took the gospel message to the remote frontiers. Many held meetings in camps where fervent prayers were offered and hymns were sung. The world of beliefs and ideas was changing and new faiths were being developed.

> There was change taking place in ideas about man's soul, as well as his body, in the period from the Revolution to the 1830's. The individualism of the American was expressed in his questioning beliefs about God without the danger of being burned at the stake.[11]

Recent writers of history have referred to some of the religious groups of that period in terms such as "half-wild denizens"[12] and that "emptiness of life on the frontier led emotions to find relief in wild orgies."[13]

The evangelists' main efforts were to convert people to their own particular faith. However, some religious leaders rendered exceptional service.

The religious revivalism which took place preceding the 1820's resulted in a temperance crusade in which over a million converts were made by 1834. Clergyman Lyman Beecher preached with great persuasion against intemperance and slavery. Temperance societies were formed, boycotts were enacted against stores selling intoxicants.[14]

People were concerned more about the welfare of the souls of their children than protecting them from the evils of child labor, which was considered an economic necessity.

Business ethics were not the province of the church. One made money to the glory of God, and possession of wealth indicated, all other things being equal, that God had smiled upon man's efforts.[15]

Not all religionists were radical—that is, strong fundamentalists or intellectual liberals. In my search for resource material that would give broad information about the people and their thinking in the period under consideration, I read with interest *The Introduction to the Critical Study and Knowledge of the Holy Scriptures,* published in 1818.[16] I was particularly interested in finding what resources were available to Joseph Smith that might have contributed to his thinking in relation to the revelatory experiences he had, especially in regard to the Utopian or equalitarian concepts which came through those experiences.

Revelation

In this connection, I have read carefully *The View of the Hebrews* and *Spaulding's Manuscript* which some have considered source material for the Book of Mormon. Neither of these, in my opinion, has any relationship to the writings of Joseph Smith, Jr.

I did find this interesting position taken by Thomas Hartwell Horne regarding revelation:

It cannot be reasonably denied that *God can, if He sees fit, communicate his will to men in a way of extraordinary revelation,* so

He can do it in such manner as to give to those, to whom this revelation is originally and immediately made, a full and certain assurance that it is a true divine revelation. If any credit be due to the general sense of mankind in every age, we shall scarcely find *one that believed the existence of a God who would not likewise believe that some kind of commerce and communication subsisted between God and man.*[17]

While there were various groups of people just preceding 1830 who were motivated by the desire to improve society, few—if any—left greater impact on the world than Joseph Smith, Jr. His encounter with Deity was most impressive and, to those who have had spiritual experiences in their own search for truth, assurance of its divinity is reflected in his testimony:

I saw a pillar of light exactly over my head, above the brightness of the sun; which descended gradually until it fell upon me. . . .

When the light rested upon me I saw two personages (whose brightness and glory defy all description) standing above me in the air. One of them spoke unto me, calling me by name, and said (pointing to the other) "This is my beloved Son; hear him."[18]

The conviction of the reality and divinity of his experience caused him to proceed with the task of organizing the Church of Jesus Christ of Latter Day Saints, the principles and provisions of which were revealed to him from time to time. These have stood the tests of attacks made against him and the church he was instrumental in founding.

The acceptance by his son, Joseph Smith III, was premised on an equivalent testimony of response to the Spirit of God, as he became president of the Reorganized Church of Jesus Christ of Latter Day Saints. Although a boy of twelve when his father was martyred, he had been close enough to those associated with his father to form opinions as to his own course in life in relation to the church.

At the time of his address to the conference of the Saints held at Amboy, Illinois, April 6, 1860, he stated:

I would say to you, brethren, (as I hope you may be, and in faith I trust you are, as a people) that God has promised his blessings upon, I came not here of myself, but by the influence of the Spirit. For some time past I have received manifestations pointing to the position which I am about to assume.

I wish to say that I have come here not to be dictated to by any men or set of men. I have come in obedience to a power not my own, and shall be dictated by the power that sent me.[19]

The contributions made by and through these two presidents of the church were of great significance and delineated the doctrines, beliefs, and principles upon which the church was to advance the cause of Christ in the realm of missionary work in preaching Christ's gospel and in the organization and development of its members in the establishment of Zion.

The conditions created by technological, industrial, and scientific development of the years just preceding 1830 required the sublimation of talents, time, and resources for their amelioration. The distinctives and goals of the Restoration Church gave incentive and direction to all those seeking to improve the status of society. It is my purpose to discuss those conditions and goals both in respect to the past and the present.

Inez Smith Davis states them somewhat idealistically:

Our critics have missed more than all else this Zion-melody in their telling, perhaps because its notes have not been clear enough, but the fact remains that without it, the story would scarcely be worth telling, for the greatest heritage we have from our fathers who wrote the story of their faith in blood and tears is the belief that this *leitmotif,* this plea for universal brotherhood, will someday rise at last to a grand triumphal chant—the glorious finale which has been the dream of our youth, the goal of maturity, and the heart's longing of our aged ones through three long generations—"the redemption of Zion."[20]

Looking Back

The change which took place from the time of the

settling of the Pilgrims in 1620 affected every phase of individual and community life. One hundred and fifty years after the time of the first permanent landings of the English in New England, settlements were scattered along the eastern coast.

Some two and one-half million people settled along a thousand miles of beachhead. Penetrations westward seldom exceeded one hundred miles. Several New England commonwealths accounted for approximately one-third of the people. A considerable number—possibly one-tenth—lived on Long Island, in New York City, and as far north in the Hudson Valley as Albany. Fort Schenectady, seventeen miles west, served as an outpost against the Indians. Pennsylvania had more people than Maryland, and Maryland had more than all New York.

There was no unity among the people. In fact, outright distrust existed between the New Englanders and the Albany Dutch. The English in New York were disliked by the Germans of Pennsylvania. Each thought the other stubborn, mean, and morally unfeeling. The Virginians thought themselves superior to others but were at the same time espousing the cause "to take their equal station among the nations of the earth."

Pre-Revolutionary immigrants had come in great numbers in the middle of the eighteenth century. Now, after almost a century, they and their families had become thoroughly American. From the first census in 1790 (population 3,929,213) to 1825, only about eight thousand a year came to America, and they were quite easily absorbed. After that time, however, the numbers increased annually from 10,000 to nearly 300,000. From about 1830 the employers of labor had available about 50,000 new hands a year. After another decade this rose to over 100,000.

During the seventeenth century the colonies were largely

English, but in the eighteenth century the immigrants were chiefly of other races with nearly all the countries of northwestern and central Europe being represented. An important—though not large—French element had been introduced through the coming of the Huguenots, who were especially numerous in South Carolina and New York. While a few Germans came to America with the Swedish and Dutch settlements, it was not until the founding of Pennsylvania that any considerable number arrived.[21] Many more arrived between 1709 and 1727 from Bavaria. In 1710 Swiss Mennonites, Palatines, Dunkers, and members of other sects came directly to Pennsylvania and settled.

The multitude of these sects were a factor in America, making a great contribution to civilization by providing for complete religious liberty, a secular state with free churches.[22]

By 1775 there were 500,000 Negroes, making up one-fifth of the population. Four-fifths of these were in the colonies south of Pennsylvania. One-third of the population in 1775 were immigrants.[23] By 1800 half a million Americans had settled beyond the Alleghanies—in Kentucky, Tennessee, and along the Ohio, often in conditions as primitive as those of their Saxon ancestors.[24]

People

A review of population trends and growth in the period preceding 1830 reveals why the United States was different from any other nation. It was indeed becoming the "melting pot" of the world.

In writing to friends in the Old World, Benjamin Franklin tried to explain the American stance: "No one inquired, 'What is he?' but 'What can he do?' "

Johann David Schoepf, in "Travels in the Confederation," wrote:

People think, act, and speak here precisely as it prompts them, the poorest day laborer on the bank of the Delaware holds it his right to advance his opinion, in religious as well as political matters, with as much freedom as the gentleman or the scholar. . . . Rank of birth is not recognized, is resisted with a total force.[25]

The period from 1776 to 1830 was a significant one. Now a new attitude of optimism was arising. Mitchell Wilson in his book, *American Science and Invention,* described it:

In 1830, Americans boasted: "The Yankee nation can beat all creation!" . . . The high hopefulness of the 1830's was due to the resurgence of the democratic spirit fifty years after the Revolution. The Republic had finally settled down with sure confidence that it would go on forever.

The 1820's had been a time of depression for many Americans. They had been frightened by the treatment they were given by the rich. By 1830 their fear had become anger. They made Jackson President: and then made Jackson the kind of man they wanted.

Wilson also analyzed the American dream of the future. It was to be achieved through four avenues—politics, economics, religion, and science. I quote two of these (and I can't help wondering why there should have been such a gap between advancing science and religion, because people were affected by both):

A third way to salvation was through religion. American ministers of the nineteenth century preached eighteenth century rationalism with the emotional fervor of the great Methodist revival of 1800. Between 1800 and 1830, this religious surge had spread throughout the nation, permeating the writings of the scientists, sustaining the struggling inventors of the thirties like Goodyear, Morse, and Howe, with the belief that an all-seeing Providence would guide them to success.

The fourth road was through science. Americans believed the great natural truths of the world were being revealed to men through God's goodness. When all the secrets had been revealed, then men would live in perfect peace and perfect happiness. Interest in science on a popular level was widespread.

It was during the period just preceding the "bringing forth" of the Restoration church that all which had transpired in the way of technical knowledge accelerated to the point where inventions and economic progress were greater than during any comparable period of civilization. This had a definite bearing on the church, its objectives, and their relation to world conditions.

Trades in America

Prior to 1770 crafts in the new land were relatively few and restricted to certain fields. One of the main categories was whaling and fishing. These called for the use of ships, boats, draggers, traps, and nets.

The Colonies were permitted by Britain to supply only raw material. Such was to be shipped to England for processing. This British mercantile theory made it practically impossible for local manufacturers to succeed. Much of the work was done in the homes. Glassblowing and papermaking were primitive because of the limitation of tools, equipment, and an outlet for marketing.

Among America's craftsmen were hatmakers, candle-makers, printers, blacksmiths, sailmakers, ropemakers, carpenters, pewterers, and tanners. For decades the general level of mechanical workmanship was of low quality. Robert Fulton, when building the "Clermont" in 1806, was able to find only one mechanic in all the city of New York capable of building a time-fuse torpedo.

Inventions—Transportation

Steam power for river craft was developed by the end of the eighteenth century. Fulton's "Clermont" made a voyage up the Hudson in 1807. Two years later, John Stevens built a steamship which he operated on the Delaware. Others were making comparable contributions in transportation.

Canals became an important segment of the transportation system. The first canal was built in South Carolina; work was started in 1793 and finished in 1800. It was engineered by Christian Sent, who was brought over from Sweden. There were no American engineers at that time. The labor force was made up of 110 slaves and freemen, one-third of whom were women working for fifteen pounds a year.[26] The greatest such project, the Erie Canal, was started under the leadership of Dewitt Clinton, an American statesman; three experienced land surveyors—James Geddes, Benjamin Wright, and Charles Broadhead—officially were made the first American engineers. The project was started in 1817 and finished in 1825.[27]

Other developments in the area of transportation were taking place also. In the decade before, post roads increased in mileage from 2,400 to 20,000 miles.[28] ("Posts" were relay stations along a fixed route which furnished fresh riders and horses for the delivery of mail.) A new bridge across the Charles River at Boston was erected a few years later. America's first iron suspension bridge was built across Jacob's Creek in Western Pennsylvania.

Railroad building had its beginning in mines and quarries, but in the years following the canal-building, self-trained American engineers began building short lines radiating out of Boston. Until 1840 train coaches were modeled after carriages of the time and were about as uncomfortable.[29] The standard American railroad car was designed after 1840 with no great change until 1870 when the Pullman was built.

These developments were born of necessity. Overland travel in the beginning of the nineteenth century was for the most part slow, strenuous, and dangerous. Roads linking population centers near the East Coast were full of potholes, ruts, and in some areas stumps.

The West was laced with a network of long, navigable rivers that made travel and the shipping of goods possible. After the steamboat appeared in western waters in 1811, the transport of passengers and cargo became feasible north and east, south and west.

Inventions in the period covered by the Industrial Revolution were of great significance and, of course, were basic to the industrialization of the country. One of the inventions which made great impact on the nation during this time was Eli Whitney's cotton gin (1794). Of almost equal importance to the nation was his mass production of the musket. Both of these inventions were accompanied by the development of tools for the manufacture of basic parts which contributed to the establishment of factories.

It was a period when "the law of simultaneous invention" made uncertain in some instances who was the originator. Such was the case of the harvester, the thresher, and the grain-binder, but—

Whatever the claims and the counter-claims, it was Cyrus McCormick who made his name synonymous with farm implements. At the age of twenty-two, McCormick had invented a hillside plow for his father's Virginia farm. The elder McCormick had spent twenty years trying to construct a reaping machine, but finally it took his son's ingenuity to develop one.[30]

Oliver Evans, a shopkeeper and mechanic, had dreams of making a horseless carriage as early as 1773, but he received little support. Later he developed the first automatic flour mill. In 1804 he was given an order by the Philadelphia Board of Health for a steam engine to be used in dredging and cleaning docks. Just preceding his death in 1819 he wrote:

The time will come when people will travel in stages moved by steam engines, from one city to another, almost as fast as birds can fly, fifteen to twenty miles an hour.[31]

Two other significant inventors of that period were Samuel B. Morse (telegraph, 1837) and John Deere (plow, 1833). The sewing machine was developed by several—Howe in 1838 and Singer a few years later. Gas lamps were a laboratory novelty at the beginning of the nineteenth century.

Although the rubber tree had been discovered as early as 1735 by a party of French astronomers on an expedition to Peru, its useful development came later. Joseph Priestly used it as an eraser when writing manuscripts. Elastic for suspenders and garters, proofing for coats, boots, and overshoes were other early uses.

Rapid progress was also being made in printing. The manufacture of paper by a new process which lowered the cost was introduced in Europe in 1803. Newspapers became popular. By 1833 there were three times as many newspapers in America as in England. That year also marked the advent of the "penny paper," the first of which was the *New York Sun*. Along with the expansion of the newspaper business there also was a comparable rise in magazine production.

Factories—Industry

The development of the factory system was the outgrowth of what had happened in England as well as in America. In the eighteenth century it was customary in England for indentured servants to be bound to their masters, who boarded them for a period of from four to seven years. As more goods were produced requiring more employees, a division of labor was essential, with each worker being assigned specific tasks. Whitney's American System of Manufacture required such a division. The English factory system was comparable.

Arkwright was the first man to drive primitive spinning wheels and looms by belts attached to waterwheels.[32]

While attempts had been made previously to introduce factory methods in America, it was not until 1787 that the first cotton mill was built in Beverly, Massachusetts. In 1814 power machinery was used to convert cotton into cloth—all within the walls of one building. This was in Waltham, Massachusetts. In 1830 a woolen factory was founded at Lowell, Massachusetts.

With the development of factories, there came benefits to the New Country—in better goods, increased commerce, growing communities by way of immigration, thus providing more workers. On the other hand, it brought about child labor, more demand for slaves, untoward working conditions that created great social problems.[33]

Robert L. Heilbroner gives a graphic description of the evils of child labor in factories:

And just as the interior of the cities provided an unlovely sight . . . interior of the new factory itself presented a still unlovelier one. For manning the new and marvelous machinery were thousands of children, concentrated, of course, in the lighter trades, such as cotton spinning and weaving. There they had been sent, in spite or desperation, by parents who would not or could not afford to keep them at home. When a tender-minded but indigent mother tearfully questioned what would happen to her child, she was easily reassured by the parish official (who often enjoyed a contract with the manufacturers to supply them with children) that at the mills they would be transformed into little ladies and gentlemen, would eat roast beef and plum pudding, would ride their masters' horses, and have silver watches and cash in their pockets.

In fact, they were shipped in lots like cattle, and sometimes no record was even kept of where they went. At the factories, conditions were all too frequently harsh and occasionally cruel to the point of being macabre.

Before 1815 there was the beginning of labor organizations among the skilled workers, and strikes became effective. The Boston carpenters walked out in 1825 demanding a ten-hour day and overtime pay. By 1830 there was the beginning of a real labor movement, uniting the workers for economic and political objectives.

Slavery

Slavery constituted one of the greatest of social evils in the settling of America. The Colonists experimented with using Indians as slaves, but this did not prove successful, so Negro slaves were brought in from Africa. Dutch traders had delivered approximately twenty in 1619. By 1700 slavery was commonly accepted as an economic necessity and traffic was even carried on by Puritan sea captains of New England. This helped some to overlook the ethics of such a practice.

The importation of Negroes was unchecked until the time of the American Revolution. It was a controversial issue throughout the Constitutional Convention which met May 14, 1787; here it was agreed by the Southerners, after much discussion, that the importation of slaves should cease after 1808. It remained an issue throughout the years of the period of the Industrial Revolution and was not resolved until the Civil War, which brought emancipation.

Southern cotton producers and factory owners required more and more laborers. They defended their position on slavery by calling it an economic necessity; at the same time they pointed the finger of scorn at the North where they referred to unemployed people in industrial areas as "wage-slaves." New attitudes were slow in developing. Jefferson saw the possibility of the Negro, if placed in the white man's environment, becoming his equal. Calhoun in the next generation took the position that "manual labor was the proper work of slaves and slavery was a positive good." It was in Calhoun's time that Joseph Smith, Jr., wrote to political leaders (including Martin Van Buren, Lewis Cass—neither of whom answered—and J. C. Calhoun and Clay) regarding his opposition to slavery. In brief, the content of his letter was a petition to

... abolish slavery by the year 1850, or now, and save the Abolitionist from reproach and pain, infamy and shame. Pray Congress to pay every man a reasonable price for his slaves out of the surplus revenue arising from the sale of public lands and from the deduction pay from the Members of Congress. Break off the shackles from the poor black man and hire him to labor like other human beings, for an hour of virtuous liberty on earth is worth a whole eternity of bondage.[34]

Joseph Smith's letters contained other suggestions for social ameliorization, such as pardoning convicts in the penitentiaries; penalizing wrongdoers by having them work on roads and other public projects; removing the practice of imprisoning people for unpaid debts; and turning penitentiaries into seminaries of learning.

Early in the century the controversy over slavery was becoming more pronounced in Missouri Territory. In 1810 there had been three hundred slaves in the Territory; by 1820 the number had increased to ten thousand (the total population was 66,000). In 1818 there were eleven slave states and eleven free states. The history of Missouri's acceptance as a state in 1820 was marked by controversy over the question of slavery. This issue was partially resolved in the fact that Missouri Territory was geographically more suitable for diversified farming than for raising cotton and thus did not require the number of field laborers that other southern states needed. Human values finally became paramount.

The increase in the number of slaves brought greater support for slavery as an institution of the South (from a million and one-half in 1820 to 3,000,000 in three decades).[35] The Abolitionists and the intellectuals of the North opposed slavery vigorously—the Abolitionists on religious and humanitarian grounds, the intellectuals because they considered it a breakdown of moral law.

Slavery was the very antithesis of the philosophy of the Restoration church, particularly in light of the revelations regarding free agency. No slave had the right of agency—neither did women or children who were bound to factory owners in the North.

Education and Social Progress

The spread of education in the United States was, in a sense, an anomaly, in view of the illiteracy which was prevalent in so many of the areas of the rapidly growing country. However, despite slavery and the increase of slums in the industrial cities, there was an underlying yearning on the part of many people to achieve the ideals set forth in the Declaration of Independence. The worth of the individual became increasingly recognized. This was true of both those who were educators and those concerned with health.

Where eighteenth century Londoners had visited Bedlam to find amusement in the poor lunatics gibbering in their chains, doctors were now beginning to consider the insane not as beasts but as human beings suffering from disease.[36]

Dr. Benjamin Rush was the leader in America in helping the mentally afflicted; he insisted on freeing lunatics from filthy cells and required those who looked after them to have formal training as nurses and orderlies. He published the first American treatise on mental disease. Others, such as Dorothea Dix—a young schoolteacher—made better care of the insane her Great Cause. After investigating state facilities in 1843 she called legislators' attention to "the present state of insane persons confined within the Commonwealth in cages, in closets, cellars, stalls, pens . . . chained, naked, beaten with rods, and lashed into obedience."[37]

Politics

As one reads church history of the period from 1830 to 1844, he cannot help thinking of the ruggedness and often the ruthlessness of American politics. Probably one of the most illustrative of these was the campaign in 1844 between Polk and Clay.

It was the closest presidential election yet in terms of the popular vote, and the most fraudulent. In New York, Tammany transformed 20,000 aliens into citizens just before election day; and in Louisiana a boatload of Democrats steamed upriver and voted in three separate towns. Not counting New York's 26 electors, Polk received 134 electoral votes to Clay's 105. Polk won the Empire State by only 5,106 popular votes, with 15,812 going to Birney, the Liberty Party candidate. Thus, had it not been for Birney, Clay would probably have carried New York and become President.[38]

Democratic procedures have certainly been marked by unprincipled men at various times and the desire for power by various groups took them to extremes. Today we face comparable problems on a much greater scale.

1. "... seek to bring forth and establish the cause of Zion."—Doctrine and Covenants 6:3a.
2. Lewis Mumford, *The Myth of the Machine*, Chapter 1, page 8, Harcourt Brace Jovanovich, Inc.
3. J. Brownowski, B. Mazlish, *The Western Intellectual Tradition*, Harper and Brothers, Publishers, New York, Chapter 16.
4. Carl L. Becker, *The Heavenly City of the Eighteenth Century Philosophers*, New Haven, London, Yale University Press.
5. Walter D. Edmunds, *The First Hundred Years* (1848-1948), no publishing house given.
6. Robert E. Riegel, *Young America, 1830-1840*, University of Oklahoma Press, Norman, Oklahoma.
7. *The Making of the Nation*, page 309.
8. Robert E. Riegel, University of Oklahoma Press.
9. *Ibid.*
10. *Ibid.*
11. *Ibid.*
12. *Story of Frontier.*
13. *The Epic of America.*

14. *The Making of the Nation,* page 149.
15. *Young America, 1830-1840,* page 16.
16. *Introduction to the Critical Study and Knowledge of the Holy Scriptures* by Thomas Hartwell Horne, B.D., Saints College, Cambridge.
17. *Ibid.*
18. *History of the Reorganized Church of Jesus Christ of Latter Day Saints,* Volume 1, Chapter 2, pages 8 and 9.
19. *Ibid.,* Volume 3, Chapter 12, page 247.
20. Inez Smith Davis, *The Story of the Church,* pages 9 and 10.
21. *Encyclopedia Americana,* Volume 27, page 339.
22. Frederick J. Turner, *Frontiers in American History,* Holt, New York.
23. *Encyclopedia Americana,* Volume 27, page 339.
24. *The Making of the Nation,* page 74.
25. *Ibid.,* page 91.
26. *American Science and Invention,* page 72.
27. *Ibid.,* page 73.
28. *The Making of the Nation,* page 76.
29. *American Science and Invention,* page 152.
30. *The Making of America,* page 318.
31. *American Science and Invention,* page 58.
32. *Ibid.,* page 84.
33. *The Making of the Nation,* page 151.
34. *History of the Reorganized Church of Jesus Christ of Latter Day Saints,* Volume 2, Chapter 31 (also Volume 5, pages 528-533, *Times and Seasons*).
35. *The Making of the Nation,* pages 300, 301.
36. *Ibid.,* page 158.
37. *Ibid.,* page 159.
38. *Ibid.,* page 231.

Chapter 3

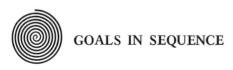

GOALS IN SEQUENCE

"Seek to Bring Forth . . ."

The commission given to the leaders of the Restoration church is crystallized in the words "Seek to bring forth and establish the Cause of Zion."

Zion was the theme of prophecy throughout the history of the Hebrew nation. The loftiest mount in Jerusalem was designated as Zion, or Sion. The whole city was thought of metaphorically as the kingdom of God on earth. It was the fortified town of the Jebusites until subdued by David, and from that time it was called the "City of David" (II Samuel 5:7, I Chronicles 11:5). Prophetic literature of the Hebrew people began with Hosea[1] and Isaiah[2] during the eighth century. Today the terms Zion and Zionism may take on different meanings with the Jewish people, but basically they have to do with the return of the Jews to Palestine. The Psalmist also wrote of Zion, "Yet have I set my King upon my holy hill of Zion" (Psalm 2:6; see also Psalms 48:12; 51:18; 69:35).

Samuel Halperin in his book *The Political World of American Zionism* wrote:

Concerning the origin of Zionism there is considerable uniformity of thinking. Beginning with the destruction of the first Jewish

Commonwealth by Babylonian Legions in the year 586 B.C. . . . longing for restoration to Jerusalem's holy mount, Zion became a cardinal feature of Jewish thought, prayer, and ritual. When in A.D. 70 a similiar fate befell the restored second commonwealth, this time at the hands of Rome, a renewed emphasis on the importance of Palestine to the Jewish people and the Jewish faith again became central to great portions of the observant Jew's daily life. History is replete with instances of Jewish attempts to regain and resettle the Holy Land; the chain of Jewish settlements in that land was never broken.

At the First World Zionist Congress in Switzerland in August 1897, the "Basle Platform," keystone of the World Zionist movement, was enunciated. It contained proposed goals as follows:

1. Promotion by appropriate means the settlement in Palestine of Jewish agriculturists, artisans, and manufacturers.

2. The organization and binding together of the whole of Jewry by means of appropriate institutions, both local and international, in accordance with the laws of each country.

3. The strengthening and fostering of Jewish national sentiment and national consciousness.

4. Preparatory steps toward obtaining the consent of governments, where necessary, in order to reach the goal of Zionism.

"All of this was subsidiary to the main objective, 'A home in Palestine secured by law.' "[3]

Around this objective there are, of course, many Zionist movements. Supreme Court Justice Brandeis stated:

The Zionists seek to establish this home in Palestine because they are convinced that the undying longing of Jews of Palestine is a fact of deepest significance; that it is a manifestation in the struggle for existence by an ancient people which has established its right to live—a people whose three thousand years of civilization has produced a faith, culture, and individuality which will enable them to contribute largely in the future as they had in the past to the advance of civilization and that it is not a right merely but a duty of the Jewish nationality to survive and develop.[4]

Just as there are diverse ideas, programs, and objectives of the Jewish people so there are parallel movements within the Restoration church. Viewing our present world situation we find that a great span exists between the ideals and accomplishments of both the Jewish people and the Restoration church.

For many years we have looked forward to latter-day Zion. We have hoped for the realization of that condition of which Isaiah wrote:

Thy people also shall be all righteous; they shall inherit the land for ever, the branch of my planting, the work of my hands, that I may be glorified. A little one shall become a thousand, and a small one a strong nation; I the Lord will hasten it in my time.—Isaiah 60:21, 22.

This would signify that a new age is about to begin. As we face our world today with the multitudinous problems which arise from war, political corruption, pollution, business avarice, the exploding population, and moral degradation, we could be inclined to question the possibility of a Zion. Yet the writings of Isaiah assure us that if we so will we can accomplish our task—the building of the kingdom of God on earth. To do this we must look to the Source of all light. Just as it was possible for Isaiah to envision that which was to come upon the earth as well as understand the conditions of his own, so is it possible for us to see "the glory of the Lord" rising upon us.

The Christ made this promise:

He that loveth his life shall lose it; and he that hateth his life in this world shall keep it unto life eternal. If any man serve me, let him follow me; and where I am, there shall also my servant be; if any man serve me, him will my Father honor.—John 12:25, 26.

Let us examine the prophecies of hope with an awareness of what their fulfillment demands of us. This can be expressed in one word—service.

Undoubtedly there have been times in the history of the human race when men have been as confused as they are today, but never in a period when there has been so much scientific development, so much in effort put forth in the interest of better human relationships, or so much improvement in the material benefits which have come through technological development. Yet these are days when the forces of darkness seem to be arrayed against the forces of Light.

Because the evil *vs.* righteousness conflict is so obvious, we should declare our allegiance to the goals which arise out of the great cause to which we have been commissioned—the Cause of Zion.

The prophetic function of the Church of Jesus Christ has been rather clearly established. There are many revelations and scriptural references which point the way for us.

Firstly, the rich and the learned, the wise and the noble; and after that cometh the day of my power; then shall the poor, the lame, and the blind, and the deaf, come in unto the marriage of the Lamb, and partake of the supper of the Lord, prepared for the great day to come. Behold, I, the Lord, have spoken it.—Doctrine and Covenants 58:3e, f.

The church is admonished again that all movements toward Zion and the gathering and temporalities connected therewith are within my law, and all things should be done in order, the advice and counsel of the elders and of the Bishop and his council be sought and honored when received, as before enjoined, though of necessity their counsel when given is not intended to dictate or to deny any man his agency. The work of preparation and the perfection of my Saints go forward slowly, and Zionic conditions are no further away nor any closer than the spiritual condition of my people justifies; but my word shall not fail, neither will my promises, for the foundation of the Lord standeth sure.—D. and C. 140:5.

I am not unaware of the skepticism relative to achieving the goals of Zion. I remember that at the time I left the F. A. Bean Company to enter church work my choice was not easily understood by those by whom I was employed. In fact the secretary of the company asked me to explain just what there was about my beliefs that caused me to assume such a responsibility. We spent hours together on a trip from Winnipeg to Minneapolis. At the conclusion of our talk—which was near midnight—he said, "Well, your ideals and hopes for Zion constitute the most wonderful story I have ever heard. There is just one thing wrong with it . . . it won't work!" Despite his comment I have never lost hope. I have seen what has happened in the lives of many people who are dedicated to this great task, and I am encouraged. My own dedication is renewed when I see the tremendous need for men to work together to change conditions which can destroy mankind if people of goodwill do not mobilize their resources to create a better world. As a church we have periodically set goals. Because of the merging and sometimes overlapping of these I have titled this chapter "Goals in Sequence."

As we consider the objectives of the church today, we need to relate them to those of the church of the 1830's. What were the basics around which the efforts of the founder and his associates were centered? I have placed them in their simplest form and categorized them in the following manner;

1. The promulgation of the gospel of Christ on a universal basis (the gospel, incorporating these principles governing man's relationship to God and to his fellowman, as exemplified in the life and teachings of Jesus Christ, recorded in the Bible, the Book of Mormon, and contemporary revelations).

2. The accepting of revelation as the guiding force in the determination of religious objectives, which objectives are

related to and give spiritual purpose in social and economic organization.

3. The attainment of broader economic equality through the orderly distribution of wealth on the basis of individual and group needs and wants (as in recognition of the individual's right of agency and voluntary action as to compliance).

4. The development of a social conscience through the sublimation of wealth (to be achieved through the implementation of stewardship in the fullest sense—the blending of mind, will, talents, and wealth to the fulfillment of the more complete enrichment of life).

5. The definition of Zion based on Doctrine and Covenants 36:2: "And the Lord called his people Zion, because they were of one heart and one mind and dwelt in righteousness. . . ."

Contemporary goals should be evaluated in relationship to these principles. They apply to man's relationship to God, man's relationship to man, and man's relationship to the world of which he is a part; they also apply to any age and any era, although needs may vary from generation to generation and may differ among races. Methods and techniques utilized in their implementation may also vary.

However, there is no substitute for love—for consideration of the poor, the underprivileged, the disenchanted, the disinherited, the lonely, the sick, and the distressed. Nor is there any substitute for trained and dedicated personnel to apply the principles in well-organized communities. By this I mean the organization of personnel and facilities to meet the needs of the community, for the community consists of individuals gathered together from various geographical areas, from all walks of life, races, and religions.

Historically it may appear to some that we have made

little progress in the direction of these goals; nevertheless, an objective study will, I am certain, show substantial progress toward their achievement. In the first fourteen years of the church (1830-1844) there were outstanding accomplishments. The organization of the church was effected in both its missionary and Zionic aspects. Not only was the organization created but broad aspects of the movement were undertaken.

Following the martyrdom of Joseph and Hyrum Smith in 1844, there were seven dark years in which groups were formed under the leadership of men such as James Strang, Lyman Wight, William Smith (brother of the prophet), William Bickerton, Alpheus Cutler, David Whitmer, and others; the largest group followed the leadership of Brigham Young.[5]

Revelations in the Doctrine and Covenants include those having to do with the calling of men for the organization of the church. Elaboration of the work to which they were called was necessary, and in December 1830 instructions were given (Section 37:2) "that they should assemble together at the Ohio." In Section 38:7a this directive was received: "And that ye might escape the power of the enemy, and be gathered unto me a righteous people, without spot and blameless: wherefore, for this cause I gave unto you the commandment, that ye should go to Ohio; and there I shall give unto you my law."

Here the revelation designated as Section 42 was given in February 1831. This contains the basic provisions of the law,[6] and its contents have been reaffirmed by subsequent revelations.[7] In it the following objectives are delineated:

1. Missionary (preaching the gospel)
2. Stewardship (agency, accountability, moral and personal disciplines)

3. Gathering (land purchase)
4. Storehouse (consecration)
5. Care of the poor and needy (equality)
6. Zion (the building up of the New Jerusalem and the Temple)

Today we hear much about the need for law and order. It is important that we emphasize the far-reaching provisions incorporated in this revelation and recognize it as the constitutional law of the church.

First, let us consider it in relation to our missionary goals as stated in Doctrine and Covenants:

> I give unto you a commandment, that then ye shall teach them [scriptures] unto all men; for they shall be taught unto all nations, kindreds, tongues, and people.—42:15b.
>
> If thou shalt ask, thou shalt receive revelation upon revelation, knowledge upon knowledge . . .—42:17a.
>
> My servants shall be sent forth to the east, and to the west, to the north, and to the south . . .—42:18a.
>
> And again, the elders, priests, and teachers of this church shall teach the principles of my gospel which are in the Bible and the Book of Mormon, in which is the fullness of the gospel . . .—42:5a. [8]

That there has been consistency in the statements and objectives of the church is evidenced by revelations and General Conference enactments. To illustrate specifically, I refer to those given in 1830 and 1831. The following two hold both promise and designation of the place of the City of Zion:

> And righteousness and truth will I cause to sweep the earth as with a flood, to gather out my own elect from the four quarters of the earth unto a place which I shall prepare; a holy city, that my people may gird up their loins, and be looking forth for the time of my coming; for there shall be my tabernacle, and it shall be called Zion, a New Jerusalem.—Section 36:12.
>
> Hearken, O ye elders of my church saith the Lord your God, who have assembled yourselves together, according to my commandments,

in this land which is the land of Missouri, which is the land which I have appointed and consecrated for the gathering of the Saints: wherefore this is the land of promise, and the place for the city of Zion. And thus saith the Lord your God, If you will receive wisdom here is wisdom. Behold, the place which is now called Independence, is the Center Place, and the spot for the temple is lying westward upon a lot which is not far from the courthouse; wherefore it is wisdom that the land should be purchased by the Saints. . . . Behold, this is wisdom, that they may obtain it for an everlasting inheritance.—57:1a-e, g.

That the breakup of the church in 1844 did not deter or diminish the hope and assurance of Joseph III and the Saints is verified in subsequent revelations. Section 128:6, 8 evidences the practicality of proceeding with the program of the gathering and the implementation of Zionic undertakings:

The great variety of callings, avocations, and professions will present difficulties precluding the practicability of all settling and living in near proximity to each other. It is therefore within the province of those upon whom the burden of organization may rest to provide for other organizations or associations than those simply pastoral or agricultural. Under this head there may be placed industrial associations of such sorts as the varied qualifications existing among workmen may demand.

The Spirit saith further: That these organizations contemplated in the law may be effected and the benefits to be derived therefrom be enjoyed by the Saints, in such enjoyment they cannot withdraw themselves so completely from a qualified dependence upon their Gentile neighbors surrounding them as to be entirely free from intercommunication with them; yet it is incumbent upon the Saints while reaping the benefits of these organizations to so conduct themselves in the carrying into operation the details of their organizations as to be *in the world but not of it,* living and acting honestly and honorably before God and in the sight of all men, using the things of this world in the manner designed of God, that the places where they occupy may shine as Zion, the redeemed of the Lord.

I am not attempting, in the delineation of the church goals and principles, to separate those following 1844 from those established in the 1820's and 1830's and up to 1844. Nor am I attempting to list them according to subject material referred to when discussing the content of Section 42. Joseph Smith III, in restructuring the church after he became president of the Reorganization, did so in harmony with the revelations received through his father. He sought to provide for their implementation in such areas as the gathering, land purchase, and the storehouse, as well as giving attention to priesthood organization and function.

As men from all directions flocked to his standard, Joseph Smith, with rare tact, constantly urging temperance, tolerance and long-suffering, made of them a united priesthood. There were difficulties, but they were few considering the situation from whence they were being slowly extricated.[9]

A brief review of the progress made by the church may prove helpful. In 1851 those adhering to the original teachings and doctrine of the church began gathering under the leadership of men such as Zenos H. Gurley, W. W. Blair, and I. L. Rogers. This resulted in the drawing together of various small nuclei in 1860, which culminated in the reorganization of the church under the leadership of Joseph Smith III, who had been designated by his father as his successor.

The period beginning with 1860 and lasting until 1914 was largely devoted to the mobilization of members and resources. During this time the reestablishment of the fundamentals of the church and the organization of its missionary work were effected. Although the Reorganization did not attain rapid numerical growth, considerable missionary work was carried on. Through the reaffirmation of the original precepts, doctrines, and beliefs of the church a spiritual philosophy was developed that served as a base upon which the church could build. It was essential that such be accomplished first and, during this particular period of time, because of the scattered condition of the members there was little opportunity to emphasize the social or Zionic phases of the work. Individual needs were of primary consideration.

I can recall that, as a small boy living in the little town of White, South Dakota, one of the missionaries visited our home. My father had been successful in getting the use of the town school building for missionary services. After a few nights of reasonably successful meetings, he was denied further use of the building. The citizens didn't want any Latter Day Saints to preach in the community because "Latter Day Saints were polygamists." My parents were given no opportunity to explain, and the series was brought to a close.

Many changes have taken place since then. The Utah church has established itself as one of the dominant religious groups in the world. While basic doctrinal differences between the Restoration churches seem irreconcilable, there are common interests, particularly in the socioeconomic areas, which make possible important contributions to human welfare.

Real problems confronted the Reorganization in its early days. The most important was that of gathering together members who were loyal to the original beliefs and doctrines. Many were disappointed and did not know which way to turn. That Joseph III was aware of this is evidenced in the admonition given in April 1877:

That the work of restoration to which the people of my church are looking forward may *be hastened* in its time, the elders must cease to be overcareful concerning the return of those who were once of the faith but were overcome in the dark and cloudy day, fearing lest they should bring in hidden heresies to the overthrowing of the work; for verily, there are some who are chosen vessels to do good, who have been estranged by the hindering snares which are in the world and who will in due time return unto the Lord if they be not hindered by the men of the church. The Spirit says "Come"; let not the ministers for Christ prevent their coming.—Doctrine and Covenants 119:4.

Fortunately, the church held together, and foundations were laid for greater work ahead. Beginning in 1915 more constructive educational efforts were started which tied into spiritual philosophy the financial and social emphases which were a part of the original doctrine of the church that had been so clearly reaffirmed by Joseph III in the revelation given in 1902 (Section 126:10).

It has been said that these emphases were out of proportion to our ability to meet the economic costs involved. It was also evident that the efforts put forth were undertaken without due preparation and consideration of the many factors involved which were essential to the success of such a broad program. Consequently we found ourselves at the beginning of the depression in 1931 under the weight of debts that had accumulated through lack of wise planning in relation to the limited financial and manpower resources available.

This necessitated reevaluation, adjustment, and careful reconsideration of the principles of financial administration, particularly in the matter of debt.[10] In looking back, we see that certain lessons have been learned. Probably the main one is that the development of a new social order requires a philosophy which has its roots in the fundamental principles and truths which have been revealed as a part of the divine plan. We have learned also that the practical application of this philosophy in the lives of individuals and groups depends on an intelligent direction of the constituent parts of the group toward the composite objective. In times past there have been intellectual differences among members which has resulted in so-called intellectualism being given precedence over so-called fundamentalism. However, the church body under authoritative ministry has clung tenaciously to the concept of a present-tense God, the divinity of Jesus, and continued revelation as basic to the emergence of a Zionic society. Such emergence depends on the development of a unity of mind and purpose on the part of the majority of the members. This has proved to be true not only in our own experience but in the experiences of other groups which have attempted to change social conditions.

Thomas Carver states:

> A society is something more than a conglomeration of individuals. It is an organized group, having a conscious purpose and, in the interest of that purpose, exercising some control over the behavior of its individual members.
>
> Their intelligence may enable them to see the superior advantage to themselves of such association . . . also that there may be emotional interests which bind them together, the interest of love of association; . . . further, that there may sometimes need be coercive pressure where some do not see the need of the first.[11]

In commenting on the philosophy of Max Nordau*, especially his *Degeneration* (D. Appleton and Company, New York, 1895), Carver has this to say:

> Among those degradationists who attribute man's low estate to the degenerating influences of civilization, Max Nordau deserves first rank because of his outspoken and unflinching pessimism, tempered, it is true, by a wholesome belief in the purgative powers of natural selection. The influence of poisons in the form of alcohol, nicotine, opium, poisonous foods, and bad air, produce a degeneration of morals and manners simply because the majority become degenerate. They give tone and set standards, they lead the fashions not only in millinery, but in politics, dramatics, literature, art, and philosophy. The sober, steady-going, sound, healthy, and sensible minority are laughed out of countenance by the degenerate mob.
>
> Thus even vice itself becomes an agent of moral adaptation by acting as a fool killer to weed out those who cannot withstand the

---

*Max Simon Nordau, German physician and author, born in Budapest, Hungary, July 29, 1849; died January 22, 1923.

degenerative forces of our complex civilization. They who can be in the world but not of it, who can keep themselves unspotted from the world, who, in the midst of the demoralizing influences of modern civilization with its great cities can remain immune to their contagion, are to survive, reproduce their kind, and build the civilizations of the future.[12]

These factors are substantially set forth by other sociologists and are certainly descriptive of the Restoration objective. Naturally there have been differences of opinion among both leaders and members of the church relative to theology, doctrine, Zionic and social concepts, but the basics contained in Section 42 have been the primary undergirdings of our church structure. It is therefore important that we examine the contemporary status of past revelations, beginning with Section 42 which has been referred to as "the basic constitutional law of the church." This has been validated from time to time:

And further the Spirit saith unto you, that "with the Lord one day is as a thousand years, and a thousand years as a day"; therefore, the law given to the church in Section 42, over the meaning of some parts of which there has been so much controversy, is as if it were given today; and the bishop and his counselors, and the high council, and the bishop and his council, and the storehouse and the temple and the salvation of my people, are the same to me now that they were in that day when I gave the revelation.—122:6a-c.

The basis of evaluation of scripture is disclosed in Section 126:10a-c given in 1902:

In regard to the gathering and the work of the Bishopric in regard to the law of tithing and consecration, I made inquiry what should be the attitude of the church in regard thereto. To this question I was answered, that the Book of Doctrine and Covenants . . . was to guide the advice and action of the Bishopric, taken as a whole, each revelation contained therein having its appropriate bearing upon each of the others and their relation thereto; and unless the liberties of the people should be in jeopardy, the application of the law as stated by the Bishopric should be acceded to.

Accountability—Stewardship—Agency

The following scriptures place special responsibilities on members of the church, as well as those who consider membership: "Every man accountable . . ." (42:5, 9; 16:6, 7; 17:20; 101:2).

The following continue as specific goals of the church of today. (These will be discussed more fully in subsequent chapters.)

The Gathering

The city of the New Jerusalem shall be prepared, that ye may be gathered in one.—42:3b, 10c; 98:10.

F. H. Edwards, in his *Commentary on the Doctrine and Covenants,* says of Section 42: "The gathering is now declared to be the very heart of the church work."

The Doctrine and Covenants contains these significant statements:

It is well to understand that the term *regions round about* must mean more than a small area of country round about the central spot.—128:5.

The church is admonished again that all movements toward Zion and the gathering and temporalities connected therewith are within my law.—140:5.

The Storehouse

. . . After this first consecration, which is a residue, to be consecrated unto the bishop, it shall be kept to administer unto those who have not. . . . Therefore, the residue shall be kept in my storehouse, to administer to the poor and needy, as shall be appointed by the high council of the church, and the bishop and his council, and for the purpose of purchasing lands for the public benefit of the church, and building houses of worship, and building up of the New Jerusalem . . . that my covenant people may be gathered in one, in that day when I shall come to my temple. And this I do for the salvation of my people.—42:10.

Care of the Poor

And, behold, thou wilt remember the poor, and consecrate of thy properties for their support.—42:8b.

No one of the poor and the needy should be neglected . . . to assist in looking after the poor and needy . . .—122:6.

An examination of the writings containing statements of policy of the late President Frederick M. Smith leaves no question in our minds as to the call and commission of this church to establish Zion. In an address to the young people on December 3, 1922, at the Stone Church he spoke of his intense interest in Zion:

It will be recalled that in the over twenty years of my ministry in this church I have been calling for preparation for Zion.

Let me say to you what I have said to the people in the Salt Valley of the West. No section of the church organized by Joseph Smith, the Seer, has as yet entered upon the chief thing that leader brought to the world, and that is the establishment of a reformed social condition that will bring about the readjustment of the evils that have crept into our present society and the preparation of a people and place wherein the kingdom of God can be established upon the earth.[13]

This sense of obligation and need is more clearly defined in this statement:

The subject of stewardships involves in its final analysis the whole social philosophy of the church; this philosophy has been taught since the church was established in 1830 and sporadic attempts have been made at times to put it into some form of practice, but no attempt has been made to have its principles generally applied throughout the whole church. This hope was warmed in 1894 by the divine instruction that Section 42 "is as if it were given today."[14]

The revelation, Section 42, which came through Joseph Smith III, covered the broad scope of the work of the church; its vital instructions included both the missionary and Zionic programs of the church.

1925

The social program outlined by President Frederick M. Smith, adopted by the Conference of 1925, incorporated these steps:

Be it resolved that we favor the immediate initiation of a program looking towards the establishment of Zion and the application of the law of stewardships, which program is as follows:

That the Bishopric secure completed financial statements by the selection of a corps of men qualified by special training (if possible) who shall be assigned territory with a view to securing these financial statements by personal contact.

That financial statements be provided which are especially designed to serve these purposes.

That the members of the church be requested to file their financial statements annually.

That arrangement for the payment of tithes due the church should be made at the time of filing the inventory.

That all who are willing and desirous should be placed upon the stewardship basis, either individual or group, as they shall manifest the essential qualifications.

That books, tracts, etc., expressing the social ideals of the church should be published without delay.

That ministerial propaganda of the church include the presentation of the social ideals of the church with specific reference to the law of tithing and consecration, that they may cooperate in the education of the Saints, particularly young people and inquirers.

That the people of the church should be urged to gauge their expenditures in accordance with definite budgets to be formulated with the idea of maintaining an equitable standard of living consistent with the attainment and perpetuation of their maximum efficiency and the needs of the group.

That in looking to the completion of the surveys of manpower, capital, markets, territories, etc., a bureau of research and service should be established.

That the determination of the order of economic development should be given immediate consideration.

That the surplus consecrated from stewardships in operation

should be set aside for, or at once used in, the establishment of other stewardships.

That, in view of the extension of our social organization, there will be necessity for providing vocational guidance and training.

Much of this program has been carried out in current procedures. The compliance of members has resulted in definite progress for the church.

1932

The next major program was approved by the General Conference of 1932. This arose out of the situation which had developed in the 1920's when the church had attempted more than it was financially able to achieve. The 1932 program approved by the Conference established both general and specific objectives. In the application of the principles of Zionic organization, leaders gave consideration to the general economic condition. A depression had begun which was to continue throughout the decade.

Objectives

The goals set forth were as follows:

1. The building of a society of people inspired with a like faith, hope, and spiritual type of life, having the materials for the daily needs of a people, from the physical and temporal aspects, is the ultimate objective placed before the church by the law. The physical and temporal aspects are but the supports for and background of a Christian life of the highest order possible.

2. This society must be provided with means of daily existence, and all steps taken must be for the purpose of providing these fundamentals in the form of food, clothing, and shelter, as well as the tools and equipment of work and production, transportation and communication. Hereunder will be included the continuance of agricultural stewardships, establishment of canneries, creameries, cheese factories, service institutions of various kinds, textile and clothing factories, among others.

During the Joint Council and Board of Appropriations

sessions of February, 1931, a financial policy was adopted, which included the following points:

1. *Arrest expansion.* Build only when present obligations have been met and necessary means are in hand to cover cost and maintenance of further work.

2. *Liquidate assets.* Turn into cash as rapidly as possible all assets not needed for the major work of the church and apply the proceeds against debts.

3. *Balance the budget.* Expenditures must be less than income, permitting a margin of safety in regular operations.

4. *Operate economically.* By stopping the leaks arising from expensive operations or from activities having a cumulatively increasing cost, major work may more certainly be done.

5. *Pay indebtedness.* By adhering to the foregoing it is possible to meet obligations. A substantial amount should be set aside each year for this purpose until the entire debt is paid.

6. *Create reserves.* This will assure economic security in the future.

Other immediate and longtime objectives were discussed and approved as goals for the church in that particular period. Included in the 1932 objectives was a program covering the major teaching objectives of the church. They are found in the General Conference minutes and also are published in pamphlet form. The following are excerpts:

1. The message of the Restoration, with its distinctive features including such principles of belief as outlined in the "Official Statement of Belief and Epitome of Faith and Doctrines" and "Belief and Practice" with especial emphasis on such features as continued revelation, divinely authorized priesthood, the Book of Mormon, and the divine mission of the church.

a. In the teaching of this distinctive message not only the application of, but the authority for, the same should be sought in "life." The message of the restored gospel must not only be expressed in individual and social living but find its essential truth in the nature of life itself. The gospel way is the way of life.

b. This distinctive message should be recognized as a direct challenge to the paganism in the present social order. We should therefore fearlessly proclaim the ethics of Christ, set up his

90

standards of value and conduct—the sinfulness of sin and the godlessness of many institutions and practices.

2. In our teaching, the major objectives of the church should always be brought into clear perspective: The evangelizing of the world and the establishment of Zion.

3. The heart of this gospel message is in true human and divine relationships, and is found in the doctrine of stewardships.

4. The "law of temporalities" should be stressed, kindly and firmly, without equivocation or apology and as impartial in application.

1947

A report to the General Conference by the First Presidency in 1947 contained this statement of the goals of the church:

1. Set up immediate and longtime programs for branches and stakes. In large and important centers, these programs will be the fruit of the labor of as many of the general officers as are necessary and can be available.

2. Pursue our missionary task in harmony with the branch and stake programs adopted and, in addition thereto, strengthen and stabilize missionary work at home and abroad, underwriting the work in distant lands as experience, necessity, personnel, and finances indicate and permit.

3. Advance the gathering with vigor while yet doing our utmost to retain in points distant from Independence those ministers and members whose services are necessary in the development of those centers.

As necessary means to these ends we further propose to

4. Make persistent efforts to elevate the standards of home and family life throughout the church.

5. Call, train, supervise, and trust local leaders. The emphasis here will be on development of local leaders and workers so as to free general officers for their distinctive tasks.

6. Give departmental work distinctive Latter Day Saint significance and integrate it with the programs of the branches, districts, and the General Church.

All of these were amplified and, in addition, emphasis

was given to procedures relative to the gathering (see page 4 of pamphlet, *Reports and Objectives of the Church*).

1966

A statement of the major objectives of the church was again made at the World Conference of 1966. This was published in the *World Conference Bulletin* of April 18:

1. *Clarify the theology of the church and unify the members in their faith.* Learning and understanding the basic beliefs of the church involves the interpretation of religious experience in all ages and leads to the determination of our theological commitments. . . .

2. *Deepen the effectiveness of worship within the church.* . . . We shall address ourselves to the task of helping our people achieve greater depth of spiritual experience through forms of worship which are indigenous to the cultural patterns of the worshipers.

3. *Develop World Church concepts and procedures in evangelism and administration.* The church in every nation must be encouraged to be self-supporting in leadership and finance. . . .

4. *Decentralize the administration of the church.* A further shifting of responsibility to national, stake, and regional levels. . . .

5. *Interpret the Zionic concept for our day in world terms and aggressively pursue the implementation of Zionic development.* There is a great need to interpret concepts about the kingdom of God and Zionic communities in a worldwide context. . . .

As a result of the experience gained during the years of the history of our church we have learned the need for a broader concept of the principles involved in the development of our own social order, and certainly we have learned the need for the development of a spiritual unity which will cement our fraternity in bonds that will enable us to be "in the world but not of it" (Doctrine and Covenants 128:8b). That we have lacked this spiritual unity in the past is apparent. The breakup of the church in 1844 was caused by dissension from within and struggles for authority and power on the part of some of the leaders of the church. This found its outgrowth in the Utah movement. Also, there were unwise declarations of intent. The kingdom was conceived by some to give them domination over their fellows and priorities in respect to land ownership and economic resources.

Subsequent to that time there were struggles for leadership within the Reorganization. Particularly was this true between 1918 and 1925. The result was schisms and withdrawals. Emphasis was laid on prerogatives and rights rather than on the responsibilities of men in places of authority.

I recall something of my own experience during those years. Because of dissentient factions in my home branch, I had concluded that I preferred to pursue other interests. Quarreling in the Church of Christ was, to me, most disheartening. However, I still maintained my interest in the church and its objectives. Each issue of the *Herald* contained articles pro and con regarding "supreme directional control." When I asked my father which side he thought was right, he replied, "Neither of them." He felt that administratively the First Presidency should have effectively clarified issues. Whether this was a valid criticism or not may be questioned by many, but where authority is vested, responsibility is equally concurrent. Leaders, to be effective, have the obligation to recognize the rights of others. Compliance with church laws is a requisite not only for members but for those in high offices as well. Common consent carries with it the right to disagree when convictions run deep, and the wise exercise of agency is imperative.

Many members were deeply disturbed during that period, and the church sustained disheartening losses. Some of the issues remain unclarified, and church progress continues to be hampered because of them. Only as the principles of the law are applied fairly to all will there be unity and progress.

The responsibility for the development of a clear concept

is first imposed on those responsible for directing the movement. Then the concept should be developed in the minds of the individual members. This can be done only through clear-cut statements of policy and the affirmative teaching of these statements on the part of the priesthood. Too often individual interpretations rather than basic principles of the law have been emphasized.

There is also need for an understanding of the processes of organization. More than at any previous time the selection of manpower is a vital problem, for only as men understand can they convey to others the concepts which are so essential to progress. Hence, those assigned certain responsibilities should be selected not only because of outstanding qualifications but also because of their clear vision and understanding of the work of the church. This does not necessarily mean highly educated men; instead it calls for those imbued with desire and equipped with special training and qualifications in certain key areas of service.

In the Zionic movement all work is honorable, and the standard of quality is high—a bit higher even than that which the world calls for. This also applies to the training of personnel.

There needs to be a clear concept respecting the relation of economic and temporal control in relation to other phases of church work. This means a clearer definition of functional responsibilities which evolves out of our common thinking. There is also need for priesthood functions (which are quite clearly delineated in the law) to be performed without restrictions imposed by hierarchical administration to the exclusion of participation on the part of those affected.

In a recent book, to which occasional reference will be made,* it is pointed out that in large industry decisions are

---

*The New Industrial State, Chapter XXVI, page 4.

made by groups, with specialists in various fields contributing to their thinking. Thus major policies and decisions involve many people.

There is a need for our objectives to be redefined and restated in the light of changing world conditions. There should also be continuous emphasis on the developing of personnel from within the church itself and drawing through missionary endeavors personnel qualified to make contributions to our social movement. I believe that there are qualified people in our church in the fields of business, industry, and the professions who are capable of resolving certain problems of management, administrative organization, and procedure while at the same time keeping within the framework of church law and organizational structure. This sets forth the thought that Zion can be achieved only as it is organized in harmony with the overall missionary and Zion-building program.

There is also a continuing need for the development of a unified spiritual philosophy paralleling a well-planned financial and economic structure for the support of the whole movement in its educational, spiritual, and economic aspects. Such a structure incorporates the provision for and establishment of the storehouse. All of the foregoing suggests the need for reevaluation of our program, goals, and objectives in the light of the basic principles which have been revealed to us. This also means separating them from traditional and unsupportable mysticism which may occasionally becloud the real issues before us.

Sometimes our movement has been retarded by those who refuse to accept leadership and seek to interpret the law without regard for the thinking of others. There are some few who hold themselves accountable only to God. Our whole philosophy is built on the idea that we are accountable to

God through accounting to the church; therefore, we are accountable to him both individually and collectively. Some ignore the wisdom of others and rely only on their own personal contact with God. While this is laudable in some cases, they should remember that truth and righteousness need to be tested in the crucible of experience.

On the other hand, man is a steward and has the responsibility of using mind, talents, and resources for the full attainment of personality. He is not expected to follow a leader blindly. He should evaluate all objectives and determine whether they are acceptable to him. In the light of the foregoing we should restudy the basic principles which establish the goals of the Restoration church.

---

1. "O Israel, return unto the Lord thy God; for thou hast fallen by thine iniquity. . . . I will be as the dew unto Israel; he shall grow as the lily, and cast forth his roots as Lebanon."—Hosea 14:1, 5.
2. "Zion shall be redeemed with judgment, and her converts with righteousness."—Isaiah 1:27.
3. *Political World of American Zionism,* 1961, Detroit University Press, pages 5-6.
4. *Ibid.,* page 8.
5. *History of the Reorganized Church of Jesus Christ of Latter Day Saints,* chapters 1-5.
6. See preface to Doctrine and Covenants 42; also statement by F. H. Edwards in *Commentary on the Doctrine and Covenants,* page 101.
7. Doctrine and Covenants 122:6, 126:10.
8. These are supported and expanded in other sections: 28:2a; 119:8a; 125:12a; 126:10; 134:5a, b; 135:4.
9. Inez Smith Davis, *The Story of the Church,* page 447.
10. See Doctrine and Covenants 18:5d; 101:13; 127:4; 130:7; 64:6; 125:16.
11. Thomas Nixon Carver, *The Essential Factors of Social Evolution,* Harvard University Press, pages 4, 5.
12. *Ibid.,* pages 99-101.
13. "The Essentiality of Loyalty in the Development of Zion," *Saints' Herald,* Volume 20, No. 2, page 25.
14. "Our Social Program," published in the *Herald* of May 13, 1925, Volume 72, No. 19, page 521.

Chapter 4

 THE QUEST FOR EQUALITY

Democracy Essential to Restoration

Throughout world history the place of the church in relation to the state has been one of the great problems confronting those in positions of leadership. At times the state has controlled religious institutions and has consequently affected the beliefs of its citizens. At other times, the church has influenced government to impose its will on the minds and the actions of its citizens.

From the beginning of the Christian movement until the Middle Ages men had difficulty in expressing themselves beyond that to which they were circumscribed by the state or church or both. To the millions of tourists who visit them the cathedrals of the Old World bear mute evidence of the influence of the church and in many instances of its power over the individual. I thought of this as I visited some in Europe, for the cost of building them was enormous both in money and human labor.

In past centuries individuals could not exercise the right of free expression without facing the censure of vested authority; this often resulted in persecution of the person and family. Men did not find free range for expression in either government or religion. This lack of freedom motivated those who were the early settlers of America to leave

97

their native lands. They came from Holland, England, Germany, and other countries, and their coming made possible the establishment of a government based on individual and inherent rights.

Despite the lack of civil and spiritual freedom in the Middle Ages, there were those who could not be suppressed. When one reviews history preceding the discovery of America, he sees the outreach of the mind into the realm of the unknown—in science, in research, and in other fields. Columbus the navigator believed that he could reach the Far East by sailing westward around the world. In the process of proving his belief, he had to surmount poverty, and indifference, and skepticism—both before and during his journey. Despite rebellious crew members, he kept his courage until they reached the new world. Here he found people with traditions that indicated their Israelitish origin. It is to these that we point as evidence of the authenticity of the historic record contained in the Book of Mormon.

One hundred and twenty-eight years after Columbus made his historic voyage the Pilgrim Fathers sailed to this new country. The settlements which were established subsequently were made up of different groups with varied motives. Some came to the new country to escape political persecution, others to find religious freedom. In addition America held out prospects for greater economic freedom, rewards for labor expended, and hope for bettering their material condition. Trading companies were organized to sponsor and finance settlements; these also contributed to the growth of the colonies.

Following the development of the colonies there was a time when one of the most important documents in the history of the world—the Declaration of Independence—was written. In it the principles of freedom and democracy were enunciated:

We hold these truths to be self-evident [said these framers of the Declaration]: That all men are created equal; that they are endowed by their Creator with certain inalienable rights; that among these are life, liberty, and the pursuit of happiness.

From this came the Articles of Confederation, which formed the basis for the early colonies to stand as an independent nation in a new world. These were followed by the writing and the enactment of the Constitution, a document described by the English statesman, Gladstone, as "the most wonderful work ever struck off at a given time by the brain and purpose of man." Thus a basis was established upon which men could more fully express their religious concepts and move toward God-given goals. Finally the ideals so long pursued were being summarized in a democracy. Through the newly formed government, churches had opportunity for more complete expression of doctrine, theology, and social reform, although the diversity of opinions often led to animosity which proved detrimental to both spiritual and social progress. Nevertheless, a climate was created wherein these differences could be expressed with growing assurance of the protection of individual rights.

Since the beginning of the Restoration movement, many changes have taken place, particularly in recent decades. World War I brought four years of destruction, bitterness, and despair. For a time following it Old World governments were confronted with new tasks of solving social and economic problems. I well remember my own feelings in November 1918. Democracy had been preserved for the future, and we hurried back from military service to take our places in civilian life—confident that all would be well. Soon, however, we found new difficulties arising.

Old World governments that had a sense of unity and solidarity put forth efforts to meet the problems and at the same time to preserve the ideals of democracy. In other nations, the desire for liberty and the right to vote were sacrificed to central control in the hope of achieving security. These conditions led to another world crisis and World War II. A lust for power, the ideology of superior races, and the degradation of human life were pitted against the basic principles of love, justice, equality, and human rights. Christian ideals survived only to be confronted by the communistic philosophy, which brought with it the regimentation of men and material resources. The purpose of this regimentation was not to liberate people but to control them.

From its very inception, democracy has been based on belief in God. From the time of the Pilgrims up to the present, in our governmental assemblies—national, state, and municipal—we pay homage to and recognize God as the Creator and Ruler of all.

In his inaugural address President George Washington said:

Such being the impressions under which I have, in obedience to the public summons, repaired to the present station, it would be peculiarly improper to omit in this first official act my fervent supplications to that Almighty Being who rules over the universe, who presides in the councils of the nations, and whose providential aids can supply every human defect, that His benediction may consecrate to the liberties and happiness of the people of the United States a government instituted by themselves for these essential purposes. [1]

Thomas Jefferson stated:

Let us then, with courage and confidence pursue our own Federal and Republican principles, our attachment to union and representative government kindly separated by nature and a wide ocean from the exterminating havoc of one quarter of the globe, too high minded to endure the degradations of the others; possessing a chosen country, with room enough for our descendants to the thousandth and thousandth generation; entertaining a due sense of our equal right to the use of our own faculties, to the acquisitions of our own industry, yet all of them inculcating honesty, truth, temperance, gratitude, and love of man; acknowledging and adoring an overruling Providence.[2]

As I think of democracy and of the sacrifices that have been made for it, I recall the words of Abraham Lincoln, who in his historic speech at Gettysburg, said, "Four score and seven years ago our fathers brought forth upon this continent a new nation, conceived in liberty, and dedicated to the proposition that all men are created equal."

In those early years, the nation was more nearly self-contained. The vast country to the west was our undeveloped empire. We were not closely associated with the Old World, and their governments imposed little restraint on us or our way of life. The emergence of our country as a world power and our responsibility to the rest of the world was most notably recognized by Woodrow Wilson in his League of Nations concept. The theme of it was initiated in his address to Congress on January 8, 1918:

We are provincials no longer. The tragic events of the thirty months of vital turmoil through which we have just passed have made us citizens of the world. There can be no turning back. Our own fortunes as a nation are involved whether we would have it so or not. And yet we are not the less Americans on that account. We shall be the more American if we but remain true to the principles in which we have been bred. They are not the principles of a province or of a single continent. We have known and boasted all along that they were the principles of a liberated mankind.[3]

We wish only to accept a place of equality among the peoples of the world—the new world in which we now live—instead of a place of mastery. . . . A general association of nations must be formed under specific covenants for the purpose of affording mutual guarantees of political independence and territorial integrity to great and small states alike.[4]

Today we question the meaning of democracy. What is it? I presume there are as many definitions as there are writers, but always there is the common understanding which

101

points toward human equality and religious freedom.

Democracy does need definition, but it needs more than that. It needs understanding, for it has to do with rights, and rights are essential to man's intellectual and spiritual freedom and growth.

As a religionist I believe that human rights can be protected and expanded best through a continued search for God and truth; further, that God is the source of light and of power, and that as man applies revealed truth to social problems he will grow in mental, physical, and spiritual stature.

Religion is the dynamic by which civilization perpetuates itself or in failing to serve may ultimately destroy itself. History has shown that it is just as possible to use religion and religious institutions to suppress as to enlighten and liberate men.

All religions and racial groups should have equality in relation to the rights which democracy provides for its citizens. Those who may feel that they are the "chosen few" have no priority in the God-given rights intended for all men. I think, however, that "one united church" is neither possible nor wise. The present ecumenical movement could ultimately require an acceptance of a central leadership which in turn could result in a state church—this despite the affirmations of some that all who are "believers" in Christ constitute the church. I agree, of course, that many churches have wonderful objectives and insofar as possible all churches should work together for the common good.

It has been pointed out by one writer in *Life's Picture History of Western Men* (pages 224-225) that

within a short period after its establishment our republic despatched Lewis and Clark to explore the wilderness across the Mississippi. Already settlers were pouring west through the Cumberland Gap into

Kentucky, over the Alleghenies into Ohio, down the Ohio to the Mississippi, then westward in a mighty rush to the coast. Within fifty years the Americans had staked claim to the whole land of their inheritance.

In that period the image some Europeans had was that Western civilization was crude and uncultured compared to that of Europe. However, America for the most part held promise of a culture and a civilization that would equal and possibly excel many of the achievements of the Old World. Today one can see that its history, its growth, its wealth, its future is premised on the basic principles of equality, justice, and religious freedom. It has a destiny with God; however, that destiny is equally dependent on its people.

John Knox Jessup sums up this responsibility in a few words: "On America almost alone has fallen the awful responsibility of holding open the door of history against the forces of evil until freedom is born anew all over the world."[5]

What can be said about American democracy today? Has it been tarnished by the war in Vietnam, by the revolutionary actions of the few, or by the apathy of the many who do not even take time to vote? Does discrimination against minority groups and the existence of poverty among millions prove its failure? To these questions there will be different answers. I still have faith in the democratic process and in the ultimate amelioration of wrong, but I am not so naïve that I fail to recognize the need for a revitalization of the spirit of our forefathers. Our freedom, our religious hopes and ideals are at stake. The church as an institution through which we express our faith in God, our love for humanity, our hope for a better world can thrive only under a benign and protective government. It was under such a government that the Restoration church was founded. Although at times persecution by irresponsible people threatened its existence, these were not the great mass of American people nor the government.

Evaluation Equality

One of the early objectives of the Restoration church was that of bringing about more equal conditions among men, particularly in relation to temporal things (Doctrine and Covenants 51:1). This had to do with the organization of people in harmony with laws relative to the use of temporalities and may be summarized as "All men equal according to their families, according to their circumstances, and wants and needs." Furthermore, this was to be considered in the matter of inheritances.

The social philosophy of the Restoration church filled a need which had become increasingly greater with the development of industry which called for many hours of labor, including child labor and slavery, and made for conditions which revealed the obvious inequities and inequalities that existed not only in America but throughout the world.

The church was primarily concerned with eliminating poverty and giving every man the opportunity to improve his situation. The root problem in achieving these goals was the accumulation and equitable distribution of wealth. The world today is in a constant state of turbulence because of the threat of war, overpopulation, and the possibility of food shortage for millions of people. In the last few decades underdeveloped nations have been in the forefront of the thinking of statesmen who represent prosperous and powerful countries. The great powers must of necessity carry the burden of wealth distribution to meet the needs of these underprivileged peoples.

What the future holds for the world remains to be seen, but the struggle for greater equality among the nations will continue. The competition for wealth and economic resources among the great powers and the need for alignment of nations with kindred objectives has created greater tensions than have ever existed before.

A nation such as India exists from day to day, continually on the verge of collapse. Articles in newspapers and periodicals graphically portray the effects of such poverty. Riots and strikes are commonplace with hunger an ever present specter.

Israeli-Arab problems continue to increase and receive much discussion in the United Nations. The quest for equality among the millions there who are affected will be difficult to attain.

As a church we have been like others to whom George Harris referred in his book, *Inequality and Progress,* written at the close of the last century:

> Equality is a charmed word. It fascinates reformers. . . . When the word can no longer be used indiscriminately, it is still retained as defining an indispensable principle of progress. . . . Almost every social theory gets it in somewhere as a fundamental condition of human welfare. . . . Before social and political theories are constructed, primal truths concerning the constitution, inheritance, and differentiation of men should be recognized. . . . As knowledge of history gives broader views, with moderate expectation of sudden changes, so knowledge of the laws of human selection and inheritance, which lie beneath the movements of history, corrects theories through adjustment of facts.

Practically every social movement in the history of civilization has had its origin in the desire to improve the condition of the larger numbers of society. The forces which have played one against the other have represented different interests, particularly in the economic sense. The objectives sought have been those of greater control, as well as the accumulation of monetary and physical resources. Thus in agriculture a struggle has been waged between the impoverished peasants and the landlords. In the industrial world there has been the struggle of labor against capital.

Today, some countries face the problem of millions of people being dependent on the production of wheat and rice, but they lack the equipment, experience, and technical knowledge necessary to supply the needs of their rapidly increasing populations. As a result of continued deprivation many of these people have lost the will to struggle for a better life. One cannot help asking, ·Will it be possible to lift these millions to a level of living that will be conducive to good health? This is a world task and the immensity of it staggers the imagination. Yet men of goodwill—scientists and educators as well as ministers—are working toward its accomplishment.

Social Unrest

The underlying causes of social unrest have rarely been well understood either by those who were seeking to improve conditions or by those who were trying to defend the positions of strength and security in which they found themselves. In many instances this lack of understanding has proved detrimental to those honestly and sincerely seeking to bring about a better world. Evidence of this has been most noticeable in militaristic nations which have been formed by people grasping at any straw which seemed to hold hope of a more tolerable life.

The Search for Equality

The concept of equality is not new, but the particular approach that we as a church are making to it is somewhat different from former attempts at reform. This should result in some tangible evidence that a broader equality may be developed. We should recognize that it is practically impossible to determine a basis which is equitable within the church without setting forth our relationship to the rest of society.

Practically every approach that has been made to bring about a condition of equality has been based on the premise that equality consists of an equal sharing of material goods as well as citizenship rights. This approach is fallacious if adhered to only in respect to wealth. Citizenship in the church or in society carries with it certain responsibilities, and real growth can come only when the individual assumes and discharges them. Thus real equality may be achieved only when each contributes of time, talent, and resources according to his ability.

It must also be recognized that things of the Spirit are enjoyed in greater degree by some than by others. Thus there are inequalities in the spiritual and esthetic realms as well as in the material.

Charles William Elliott, president of Harvard University, in a 1909 address entitled "The Contemporary American Conception of Equality Among Men as a Social and Political Ideal," expressed his view of inequality:

Let us now consider what human inequality does not and cannot mean. In the first place, it does not mean that men are born equal in bodily strength and vitality, mental gifts, or potential capacity of any sort. Anyone who has long been concerned with education will inevitably have become convinced that the inequalities among human beings of the same stock, as regards physical and spiritual capacities, are infinite. . . . Men, as a matter of fact, are not born equal, no two have an equal chance in life by any possibility, because their means and powers of meeting the exposures, risks, and opportunities of life are different. . . . A just social philosophy will not undertake to fly in the face of these facts of nature.

Freedom, therefore, does not mean equality, but inequality of condition among the members of a free society; and this result has been actually attained under all the free governments of the world, and nowhere to so striking a degree as in the United States. . . . The structure of democratic society will, therefore, remain full of inequalities.

The Need for Determining a Basis of Equality

The church law is specific in respect to the basis on which equality is to be established. While the law includes concise statements regarding equality, there is considerable difference between an exposition of the law and the problem of putting into operation the principles on which the law is founded.

It is important that we deal matter-of-factly with some of the elements to which consideration must be given in order to make progress toward such a goal. The thoughts which have been expressed by others who have attempted to explore this particular field are helpful. For example, in an article entitled "Equality," published in the *Saints' Herald* of February 27, 1907, Bishop Kelley discusses the principles. The following is an excerpt:

> The stewardship is to God, and not simply to the church. No rule of action can ever be made which invalidates the law requiring each to answer to God for his work, or that sets aside the doctrine of personal liberty of the citizen. God's children must be free; Zion is not made up of the following of slaves. This freedom, however, permits no one to live above the law, or to violate a single one of its provisions. True liberty is ever within the law, not outside.

The foregoing is a general statement, but it does present the agency through which equality may be attained. It sets forth a need for a recognition of God as the owner, and that each individual is responsible to Him for his conduct.

There is a tendency on the part of many members to think of equality as being achieved through a distribution of physical and material resources on an equal basis. In this connection, it is interesting to get a point of view such as that given in the April 5, 1955, issue of *Christian Economics*. An editorial, "Equalization of Wealth," points out the fallacy of the idea of achieving equality through a redistribution of wealth. It is too long to quote in full, but inasmuch as it presents a point of view relative to a problem basic to Latter Day Saint philosophy—*viz,* the distribution of surplus on a worldwide basis according to need—excerpts are worthy of consideration:

We are giving much space in this issue to the discussion of a subject close to the heart of many sensitive, dedicated Christians. The immediate reason for bringing the matter up is a thoughtful article in the *Christian Century,* February 23, 1955, by Dr. Creighton Lacy, distinguished scholar and former missionary to China. We unite with his deep concern for suffering humanity but take serious exception to his plea for equalization of wealth.

Pointing out that per capita income in the United States is $1700 and in China $27, Professor Lacy comments, "No individual or nation acquiescing in such discrepancy can appear Christian to the man at the bottom or in the sight of Almighty God." He also deplores " . . . from the depths of Christian conviction, the injustices and inequalities which now exist."

We understand this attitude for we too have lived and worked with starving people and on several occasions could scarcely eat the food offered to us when we boarded the plane for a trip home. We were given more meat in one meal than a month's ration in Europe at that time. Nevertheless, an examination of the facts forces us to the conclusion that equalization of incomes between individuals in one country and between the citizens of our country and the people of other countries is not the way to solve the problem so distressing to Christians, but on the other hand would destroy all hope of so doing.

The editor of *Christian Economics* then went on to point out that there are overwhelming numbers of people in other nations besides the four-to-one ratio of Chinese to Americans, and real redistribution to the people of the world would include Indians, Indo-Chinese, Indonesians, the Malayans, Asians, South Americans and Africans. Such distribution would impoverish America and do very little to raise the per capita wealth of the world's impoverished people. He pointed out that the United States constitutes only 6 percent of the world's people.

In the last few decades the United States has extended a helping hand to needy nations on a scale unprecedented in human history. A continuation of such help—despite the need and the altruistic spirit which may motivate such giving—can result in the breakdown of our own economy. Surely the principle of sharing responsibility for work and sharing costs wherever possible on the part of those receiving benefits should be applied.

Equality as set forth in the scriptures—and particularly in the revelations received at the beginning of the Restoration movement—is definitely dependent on a distribution of temporalities on the basis of needs and just wants; but there is also another factor which enters into the problem. This is that needs and just wants are in turn dependent on the individual's application of time, talents, and resources for the attainment of that which has been determined as the goals of society in relation to the church. Nevertheless, there is need for recognition of the fact that these needs and just wants must necessarily be limited to an area which is within the ability of the group as a whole.

There is also need for consideration of the social load placed on individuals and families. In too many instances there is not a fair distribution of responsibilities which are of service to the group as a whole. Too few carry the burdens of administrative and financial responsibility for the group. In my own experience in community service I have found that it taxes the ingenuity of civic leaders to find enough people to carry the load of community service.

For the members of the church the approach to equality begins with the basics of stewardship:

1. The management of time and resources.

2. The accounting which reflects the result of such management.

3. The allocation of time and resources to make one productive. (As one becomes productive he finds it possible to meet family needs—not only the everyday costs of running a home and educating his children but providing an inheritance as well: the house or its equivalent.)

4. The creating of reserves or surplus.

5. The sharing of that accumulated over and above such basic needs. (This sharing of time, talents, and money is made possible through the General Church and/or stake storehouses.)

---

1. *Messages and Papers of the Presidents,* Volume 1, page 44.

2. *Ibid.,* Volume 1, pages 310-311.

3. *Ibid.,* Volume XVII, page 8222.

4. *Ibid.,* Volume XX, page 8425.

5. *Life's Picture History of Western Man,* page 290.

Chapter 5

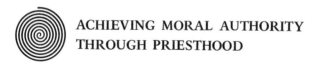

ACHIEVING MORAL AUTHORITY
THROUGH PRIESTHOOD

There are, in the church, two priesthoods; namely: the Melchisedec, and the Aaronic, including the Levitical priesthood. Why the first is called the Melchisedec priesthood is, because Melchisedec was such a great high priest: before his day it was called *the holy priesthood, after the order of the Son of God;* but out of respect or reverence to the name of the Supreme Being, to avoid the too frequent repetition of his name, they, the church, in ancient days, called that priesthood after Melchisedec, or the Melchisedec priesthood.—Doctrine and Covenants 104:1a-c.

All other authorities, or offices in the church are appendages to this priesthood; but there are two divisions, or grand heads—one is the Melchisedec priesthood, and the other is the Aaronic, or Levitical priesthood.—104:2.

The second priesthood is called the priesthood of Aaron, because it was conferred upon Aaron and his seed, throughout all their generations. Why it is called the lesser priesthood is, because it is an appendage to the greater, or the Melchisedec priesthood, and has power in administering outward ordinances. The bishopric is the presidency of this priesthood, and holds the keys or authority of the same. No man has a legal right to this office, to hold the keys of this priesthood, except he be a literal descendant of Aaron. But as a high priest of the Melchisedec priesthood has authority to officiate in all the lesser offices, he may officiate in the office of bishop when no literal descendant of Aaron can be found, provided he is called and set apart and ordained unto this power by the hands of the Presidency of the Melchisedec priesthood.—104:8a-d.

The preceding quotations quite succinctly set forth the provision for two priesthoods in the Restoration church. It is not my intent to discuss the historical background of priesthood or to delineate in detail the various functions of the offices provided. I plan instead to urge those who assume such responsibility to recognize that there is quite a gap to bridge, by way of preparation, between receiving by ordination the legal right to function and achieving the moral authority one must acquire to become an effective minister of the gospel of Jesus Christ. I am, however, including at the close of this chapter a list of references which provide helpful historical background as well as specific helps for study and development.

"For the kingdom of God is not in word but in power" (I Corinthians 4:20). The scriptures provide for a functioning priesthood through which such ministry is to be given. The church of the Restoration places great emphasis on authority and ordination in respect to priesthood.

We believe that a man must be called of God and ordained by the laying on of hands of those who are in authority, to entitle him to preach the gospel and administer in the ordinances thereof.

We believe in the same kind of organization that existed in the primitive church, namely, apostles, prophets, evangelists, pastors, teachers, and all other officers provided for in the Scriptures.—Official Statement of Belief and Epitome of Faith and Doctrine.

Authoritative Ministry Essential to Zionic Progress

Ministry begins with a divine call and ordination, and the extent to which men fulfill this call will determine their success or failure in building the kingdom. The quality of the ministerial force representing the church is therefore a most important factor for consideration.

The average person confronted with many problems growing out of our complex society will, if he is religiously inclined, turn almost instinctively to the church for direction and leadership from those who stand as authorities in spiritual realms. This, of course, has its counterpart regarding the other phases of everyday life which relate to our economic and social activities. Therefore, it behooves those who profess to have the solution to problems to recognize that authority is attained by solving existing problems as well as envisioning problems still ahead.

It is upon the premise of an authoritative ministry that we seek to build the foundation of a new society. If our claim is valid, the fundamentals of righteous living could, under such leadership, be expressed in our economic and social organizations and could result in an emerging concept that values human life above material things.

There is need for continuous development along certain lines if we are to have efficient ministers. This applies not only to those who are ordained representatives of Jesus Christ but also those who profess to be his followers. I believe that there are responsibilities which devolve upon every individual for service to Christ's church as a consequence of membership. There is no double standard of righteousness for the ministry and lay members; each is challenged to make a maximum contribution of time, talents, and resources.

There are, of course, certain qualities and abilities which one is presumed to have to justify a call to the priesthood. Then, after ordination, he is to function on the basis of the duties and responsibilities of the office to which he is called. He is placed in a position where his code of ethics will be under constant scrutiny. While he may be vested with legal authority he will find that only through experience, consecration, study, and a demonstration of fiscal, family, and social integrity will he develop the moral authority which is equivalent to the right to minister which ordination gives. I have found a variance in the codes of ethics among men, including members of the priesthood. No one is perfect, but there are moral standards to be observed which have evolved out of the experience of the human race through the centuries. In our present complex society it is even more imperative that we examine some of the bases upon which moral authority has developed. Particularly there is need for consideration of ethics and moral authority in priesthood functioning.

Ethics in Priesthood Functioning

One might well question why I give consideration to the subject of ethics in relation to priesthood functioning, when it is generally assumed that to be a good minister a man must have high ethical standards. I am interested, however, in the relationship of ministerial ethics to the development of the ideal human character in the individual minister and also the collective objective, which is the Zionic community. There are, of course, both intermediate and longtime goals. The central purpose of priesthood ministry is the development of spiritual insight to the end that what is good in man may become predominant in building a society where Christian brotherhood is expressed in business, cultural, and social life.

Ethics is defined as follows:

1. (a) The study of the general nature of morals and of the specific moral choices to be made by the individual in his relationship with others; the philosophy of morals.

(b) The moral sciences as a whole, including moral philosophy and customary, civil, and religious law. . . .

2. The rules or standards governing the conduct of the members of a profession. . . .

3. Any set of moral principles or values.

4. The moral quality of a course of action; fitness; propriety. . . .

   —The American Heritage Dictionary of the English Language

115

Dewey and Tufts in their book *Ethics* state, "Ethics is the science that deals with conduct insofar as this is considered as right or wrong, good or bad" (Introduction, page 1). This is in keeping with the preceding definition, for both deal with moral principles.

Morals are a matter of direction, not of suppression. The urgency of desires and capacities for expression cannot be got rid of; nature cannot be expelled. If the need of happiness, of satisfaction of capacity, is checked in one direction, it will manifest itself in another. If the direction which is checked is an unconscious and wholesome one, that which is taken will be likely to be morbid and perverse. The one who is conscious of continually denying himself cannot rid himself of the idea that it ought to be "made up" to him; that a compensating happiness is due him for what he has sacrificed, somewhat increased, if anything, on account of the unnatural virtue he has displayed.

It is not practicable to carry out the principle of self-denial everywhere; it is reserved for the family life, for special religious duties; in business (which is business, not morals), the proper thing is aggressive and unremitting self-assertion.—*Ethics,* pages 368, 369.

The authors go on to say that "in business the end is success, to 'make good'; weakness is failure, and failure is disgrace, dishonor. Thus in practice the two conceptions of self-denial in one region and self-assertion in another mutually support each other."

These extremes create problems of moral choice which apply most peculiarly to members of the priesthood, who are both ministers of the gospel and workingmen, living between the conflicting motivations—the self-denial required for Christian ministry and the self-assertion demanded for success in the secular world.

Moral and ethical problems arising from this involve the minister, the family, and the church. Good ethics are essential to bring about proper balance. Authoritative ministry is dependent on such decisions—or, to state it more specifically, the development by the individual of a code of ethics and living in accordance therewith makes for authoritative ministry.

From the earliest period of its history the Christian Church has regarded the scriptures as being in some sense the special revelation of God, and therefore as being in some sense the final standard or norm of Christian truth. The Old Testament seems to have been accepted from the beginning as an authoritative revelation of God, and it was not very long before the writings which came ultimately to form the New Testament were also in circulation, carrying a similar, though not precisely assessed, authority.[1]

In addition to the Bible the Restoration church accepts the Book of Mormon and the Doctrine and Covenants as scriptures. In these three books is found more material to formulate a code of ethics.

President Frederick M. Smith recognized the diverse and varied qualities of Restoration ministers. A dynamic advocate of education, he understood the problems of developing an "educated" priesthood. His first suggestion was for individual evaluation:

"Know thyself" is an old admonition, and it is by some considered the acme of educational endeavor to know accurately one's limitations—maximum and minimum. It is as pitiful to see one trying to function beyond his capacity or powers as it is to see him content to do less than his best. In either case he becomes a misfit. To know himself will keep in his consciousness his weakness as well as his strong points, and in the one case avoid temptations and in the other desist from boasting. To know oneself will require innate or acquired evaluation of mental habits.[2]

President Frederick M. Smith helped me to know something about myself. Traveling with him, as I often did, was stimulating, informative, and enjoyable. He had a tremendous fund of information in many fields. Sometimes his observations were rather critical. On one occasion we were traveling to the Ozarks to look over the "sheep

117

farming" project which the church had undertaken. While driving I involuntarily swerved the car in an obvious effort to hit a snake. I missed it, but he turned to me quickly and said, "Why did you do that?" I said, "It was a snake, I don't like snakes, and I tried to kill it." He responded by asking, "Do you try to kill everything you don't like?" I replied, "Of course not." But it set my mind at work on the evaluation of the good and bad characteristics of snakes. However, I really don't believe he was fond of them either, for a few days later he told me that a big black snake had killed his pet parakeet. When I asked him what he did about it he said, "I killed the snake." I couldn't resist saying, "I thought you liked snakes." He remembered his admonition to me and smiled.

In coming to know others, I find that I learn more of myself. I have also found that when I learn to turn over to others responsibilities that they can handle better than I, the church as a whole and both of us benefit.

That Which Makes Authority Manifest

One needs to determine the objectives of the Christian if he is to have an appreciation of the real meaning of authority, for only in so doing is it possible to set up a standard of measurement. The objective of the Christian minister is, as previously stated, the attainment of spiritual insight and power—not for self-aggrandizement but for meeting the needs of others and building the kingdom. He must also understand the importance of properly blending the spiritual and physical. Jesus illustrated the relationship between the kingdom and the righteous utilization of wealth:

For I was an hungered, and ye gave me meat; I was thirsty, and ye gave me drink; I was a stranger, and ye took me in; naked, and ye clothed me; I was sick, and ye visited me; I was in prison, and ye came unto me. . . . Inasmuch as ye have done it unto one of the least of these my brethren, ye have done it unto me.—Matthew 25:36, 37, 41.

The authority and the power of ministry is best shown in one's attitude toward others. The authority we seek comes from full obedience to the divine law and is demonstrated in one's relation to others. Those professing authoritative power will best manifest this in attitude toward, service to, and concern for their fellowmen. Legal authority, unless expressed in Christian love, has little to offer either to the one so vested or to those to whom he is to minister.

The Need for Practical Application of Principles

The Christian Church has lost much in its profession of certain legal authority because of not having made practical application of the ideals it teaches. Many an intelligent person with no religious affiliation is amazed at the lack of understanding of social righteousness on the part of those who profess to be Christians, and even more amazed at the lack of application of those principles in which they say they believe. He fails to see in them the reflection of power and authority which was so obvious in the acts of Jesus. The Master "taught . . . as one having authority." Despite this, there were those who did not accept him as the Messiah.

Jesus stated: "I am come in my Father's name, and ye receive me not; if another shall come in his own name, him ye will receive" (John 5:44) and "For had ye believed Moses, ye would have believed me; for he wrote of me" (John 5:47).

These statements of authority would not have made Jesus the Messiah, nor would they have caused men to believe in him, had they not been accompanied by practical demonstrations of divine power. He healed the lame man at the Pool of Bethesda; he turned water into wine; he fed the multitude with a few loaves and fishes. These and other miracles were evidence of the authority vested in him by his Father in heaven.

The Need for Spiritual Ministry—Moral Authority

The mission of the church has to do with life now as well as after death. The mission of the church is to bring hope and healing to those who are sick and distressed today; to bring joy and happiness to those who sorrow; and to comfort the bereaved. In addition to these, the church must develop a spiritual ministry through which there may be evidenced the power Jesus promised he would give to those who believed— the power to heal; the power to minister to mind and body and soul. These are not only the responsibilities of the ministry of the church today but they offer opportunities for those who wish to serve humanity. There is also the task of establishing the brotherhood of men, the kingdom of God.

Paul, after his experience on the way to Damascus, went out with some definite objectives in mind. The record of his life is summarized in the three great missions in which he engaged himself as he taught the fundamentals of the gospel in Galatia, Macedonia, and Asia. He consolidated groups into functioning bodies, that through them might be evidenced the entity of the church of Jesus Christ. Paul had deep conviction, and with that conviction came spiritual power which made him an outstanding representative of his Lord and Savior.

Many today wonder why the church of Jesus Christ does not evidence an authority equivalent to that of the early church. Some say we do have that authority. I feel that we have reached a point when the vocal expression of authority is not sufficient. The need is for moral authority—an authority of work and deed. The church is sustained by those willing to pay the cost, to give to it the best that they can, to function as ministers of Jesus Christ. To the extent that priesthood members are developed who are imbued with this sort of doctrine and philosophy, the church will manifest itself as the Church of Jesus Christ. Authority can come only as men bend their minds and wills to Christ and consecrate themselves to the task of ministering.

Essentials of Spiritual Ministry

One might well ask, How is this spiritual ministry to be created and sustained? How is it to exemplify and make manifest the Holy Spirit of God?

The first essential is *a desire to serve* on the part of those who would be followers of Jesus Christ. This desire must be something more than an idle wish; it must be of such a nature that it will make them willing to pay the supreme sacrifice if necessary.

But desire alone is not sufficient. It must be accompanied by initiative—the willingness to move out and assume responsibility. Men of the priesthood need to develop the ability to evaluate, to analyze, and to question when necessary programs or changes that may affect doctrine, which would in turn affect the functioning of various councils and quorums and ultimately the lives of church members as a whole. I have found that no one is infallible. Only to the extent that ministers are willing and able to discharge the responsibilities which are inherently theirs in the particular offices to which they are called will the church of Jesus Christ succeed.

Techniques of ministry must be developed. These will be based on a knowledge of human nature and psychology. There are some in the priesthood who have been satisfied with just being "called"—they have not magnified their calling or sought to improve themselves by learning; often they remain unaware of the needs of others or of their own potential ability to minister to those needs. Personal development does not, however, eliminate the need for the touch of the Holy Spirit. This gift is received only to the extent that priesthood members make preparation, seek it, and attune themselves with God.

If we are willing to conform to the revelation of divine truth which God brought to us through his Son, then we can move forward in the building of his church.

We must also have *intimate knowledge of the church,* its purposes, goals, and objectives. We must know how it is to function in its various component parts—stake, district, branch, group, family, and individual. If we know these things and understand what our task is, then we have a point of embarkation toward the achievement of the broader goals of the church, for we shall develop spiritual authority to the extent that we shall individually and collectively attain the ability to proceed with the implementation of gathering procedures, the storehouse, the further development of health facilities both in missions abroad and within the stakes. We need to understand that the concern for human life by individuals is as varied as the problems touching it.

Leadership requires the development of those qualities essential to judging current values and areas where effective ministry may be given.

Surely we have legal authority to serve but we need to match that legal authority with a moral authority that will be evidenced in the manner in which we respond to the challenge to be "in the world but not of it" using time, talents, and resources, while moving toward the alleviation of human distress and suffering "in the manner designed of God."

I Will Build My Church

If we would build the kingdom in both the material and economic sense, we must develop these attributes in our individual lives. There is reason to hope for a spiritual power that will radiate throughout the entire membership of the church and to broader sections of the human family through the ministry of those called to the priesthood of the church. Just as the Center Place functions as the economic and spiritual hub from which shall radiate the power of the authority of the church, so shall we—as we develop spiritual potency—radiate a power which will bring blessings to an ever expanding portion of the world. The sick shall be healed, the bereaved comforted, the poor will be provided for, and the principles of Zion expressed in our social and economic relations.

This is why it is essential for those who would serve to be men of strong character, integrity, and honesty. The arts of ministry must be developed both along spiritual and economic lines. Members must be taught to be productive; they must learn how to provide for themselves and also work for the church of Jesus Christ. They must labor with all of the power with which they have been endowed toward the accomplishment of the goals of the church.

Jesus is the most eminent authority regarding the things which are essential in spiritual development. Ministers of authority are those who not only look to Jesus but also—by their conduct—lead people toward him. To be authoritative they must be careful what they teach. Jesus made no mistakes. He knew his subject; his background of experience was broad; his judgment was good; and his prophetic utterances proved to be accurate.

The Need for Knowledge

As we think of the program of the church—the establishment of Zion—we should be careful of the emphasis we place on our claim as an authoritative church unless we are able to give substantial evidence of our right so to do. In undertaking the greatest task to which we can set our hand now—that of the establishment of God's kingdom—we need to know something of the essentials required in its building. It is the responsibility of priesthood to learn of and implement the economic and social framework of Zion.

The purpose of Zion is to create a condition of righteousness. The Mosaic Law served as a disciplinary influence to prepare men for the more complete law of Christ. However, it also dealt with some of the elements of social justice. These were expressed through the Hebrew prophets who not only declared God as the Creator of the earth but also emphasized man's responsibility to Him. Prophetic men like Hosea, Amos, and Malachi arose with all the strength of their spiritual and mental powers to witness that social justice was the essence of religion.

Such a study takes us into the whole field of human relationships where we encounter the need for men who can speak with authority. Surely a minimal requirement is that those who are engaged in the building of a new society should know something of the composition of present social conditions. In addition to this they will need divine guidance. At all times they should use care and wise judgment. Basic to this is an appreciation of the good in society, irrespective of the fact that it is customary to point out those things which are evil and detrimental to mankind.

In the claim that we make respecting our authority to enter into a program of kingdom building, it is important that we have substantial evidence to support our claim. There are many in the world who recognize, even as do we, that there is need for a change and are working to improve society. We shall find it exceedingly difficult to improve much on the technique of commercial and industrial organizations; in fact, we can learn a great deal from them as well as from various social movements. Progress has been achieved through the application of the principles of thrift, industry, loyalty, courage, perseverance, study, and research. These same principles must be carried over in any Zionic enterprise to assure success. Is it too much to expect that the church will continue to convert men of goodwill from business, industry, and the professions?

The Melchisedec Priesthood

More specific application may be made as we consider carefully the work of the priesthood in its functional divisions. A special ministry is conveyed to members of the church through the Melchisedec priesthood. My discussion here will be confined mainly to those phases of our movement which lie within the temporal realm, particularly the gathering.

The gathering presupposes the development of individual and group spiritual life on the part of those participating. Such can be achieved only if intelligent direction is given to members of the church. This is accomplished primarily through the Melchisedec priesthood. In this sense the elders function in pastoral ministry, which has to do with the growth of proper attitudes toward the church, toward one another as members of the family, and toward life as a whole. A point of major concern today is divorce; many of the problems connected with it could be avoided if young people were directed in the matter of marriage responsibilities. It is part of the ministry of the Melchisedec priesthood to attempt to unite divided homes—to draw into the church those members of families who have not so affiliated temselves and to teach the law in all of its varied relationships. Members of the Melchisedec priesthood should, first of all, develop competency in their vocations as well as in a knowledge of gospel principles. When they have achieved this they will be qualified to teach the membership in these areas.

The economic aspects of family life also come within the range of the teaching responsibility of the Melchisedec order.

This again relates back to the pastoral responsibility, for through it there is opportunity to give young people encouragement and to provide direction in respect to vocational activities.

Members of the Melchisedec priesthood may extend their ministry through supervision and cooperation with the Aaronic priesthood. Through their contact with priests, teachers, and deacons they can develop aids to assist individual families both specifically and generally in meeting problems.

The Melchisedec order, because of its authoritative positions in the stake, district, and branch, can retard or promote the educational program—in fact all of the activities within the church.

The Aaronic Priesthood

The Aaronic priesthood performs a distinctive ministry. In addition to administrative responsibilities the Melchisedec ministry is directed toward spiritual and educational objectives. The Aaronic priesthood is primarily concerned with visiting, teaching, and serving with emphasis on temporalities. That is why the law designates the bishopric as presidency of the Aaronic priesthood. This ministry particularly applies to the processes of the gathering and has a major responsibility, under the guidance of the Melchisedec priesthood, to bring about the coordination of the economic and spiritual life of the people.

One of the functions of the Aaronic priesthood is the teaching of stewardship in the home. This requires an understanding of home management, including budgeting and purchasing, and extends into the physical aspects of home building. It should be expected that within the Aaronic priesthood there would be those who could direct and advise church members regarding the improvement of houses and grounds.

Personal contact of these priesthood members with youth in the homes should be helpful, for through such contact the economic goals of the church could be clarified. (Possibilities of their attainment could be enhanced through the facilities of junior stewardship and other helps available from the church.) Through competent ministry, young people could be stimulated to fit themselves for vocational life and become self-sustaining.

The Aaronic priesthood could also make a contribution to the establishment of Zion and to the gathering movement by advocating certain standards of excellence in respect to occupations. Authoritative ministry requires capable performance on the part of the individual holding office. The Aaronic priesthood has the responsibility of teaching members the fundamental purposes of Zion and should be able to point out the relationship of the temporal and the spiritual aspects. This priesthood serves an important function in the church in administering certain ordinances— passing of the Communion, caring for the emblems, collecting of the offerings, etc. This requires excellence in personal appearance and an intelligent approach to those who are not members of the church.

Providing the best ministry requires a knowledge of human characteristics. Not all homes are alike, and not all individuals are alike. Members of the Aaronic priesthood should be concerned with the welfare of everyone but should have designated responsibility for ministry to a specified number of familes (not to exceed ten). Service is best rendered by those with a knowledge of the law. They should also understand the principles on which the church ministers to meet the needs of worthy members in distress.

The Aaronic priesthood may lift the standards of priestly ministry through service in the home, through the ordinances of the church, and through the contribution it may make to the improvement of the economic life of members. Priesthood becomes authoritative when it magnifies its calling through consecration and the development of skills and techniques of ministry.

The most important task is that of clarifying the duties and functional responsibilities of the various offices and quorums of the priesthood. The revelations which constitute the law and doctrine of the church seem comprehensive; however, the lack of clarification has caused most of the trouble in the church, and indecisions of the past have retarded progress.

Intensive, well-balanced educational programs for both Melchisedec and Aaronic priesthoods contribute to such clarification. Coordination of administrative groups to make possible the attainment of common objectives is, however, an underlying need in developing such programs.

More than at any time in the church priesthood education programs are being carried on and printed material is available for study. Although not everyone may agree with some of the material, it is incumbent upon all to study, to learn, to evaluate, and to broaden our perspective and understanding. I have gone through many crises in church experience in my lifetime and often have not been in agreement with authors and administrators. Nevertheless I have found strength—both spiritually and mentally—in believing in the church and its ultimate contribution to the world. When I have felt deeply about matters, I have not hesitated to express my opinion and give the basis for it. This I shall continue to do ... but the church is greater than any individual, and the Cause of Zion continues an imperative.

Helpful References

A Commentary on the Doctrine and Covenants by F. Henry Edwards (see Commentary on Section 104 of Doctrine and Covenants, page 237).

"Committee Report on Priesthood Organization" (September 4, 1969), John W. Blackstock, Chairman.*

"Presidency and Administration of Aaronic Priesthood," Linden Wheeler.*

"Zionic Procedure" (bound quarterlies), G. L. DeLapp, 1940. Authoritative Ministry—Bishopric Responsibilities—regarding temporal law, church institutions, etc.*

Priesthood Orientation Studies (Pastor's Reference Library), Herald House, 1964.

A Survey of the Doctrine and Covenants, Chris B. Hartshorn
    Chapter III—"Functions of Priesthood"
    Chapter VII—"Concerning Priesthood"
    Chapter X—"The Prophet and the First Presidency"

Exploring the Faith, Basic Beliefs Committee (paragraph 13, page 182), Herald House.

The Restoration Faith—Evan A. Fry, "What Is a Prophet," pages 263, 265, Herald House.

Priesthood Journals (these contain many articles on priesthood, e.g. "Some Things a Member of the Priesthood Should Know" by President Frederick M. Smith, Volume 9, Number 3, July 1943; "Quotations on Doctrine and Policy in the Early Church" Volume 3, Number 3, July 1937).

---

*Copies on file at Zionic Research Institute (for reference only).

1. "The Bible: Its Significance and Authority" by Herbert H. Farmer, *The Interpreter's Bible,* page 3.
2. "Some Things a Member of the Priesthood Should Know" by Frederick M. Smith, *The Priesthood Journal,* Volume 9, No. 3, July 1943.

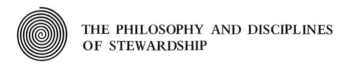

THE PHILOSOPHY AND DISCIPLINES
OF STEWARDSHIP

The philosophy of stewardship is inherent in the scriptures:

And I, God, said unto mine Only Begotten, which was with me from the beginning, Let us make man in our image, after our likeness; and it was so.

And I, God, said, Let them have dominion over the fishes of the sea, and over the fowl of the air, and over the cattle, and over all the earth, and over every creeping thing that creepeth upon the earth.—Genesis 1:27, 28 (Inspired Version).

The purpose of God's creation is set forth in a revelation given to Joseph Smith, Jr., in June 1830:

And the Lord God spake unto Moses, saying, The heavens, they are many and they cannot be numbered unto man, but they are numbered unto me, for they are mine; and as one earth shall pass away, and the heavens thereof, even so shall another come; and there is no end to my works, neither to my words; for this is my work and my glory, to bring to pass the immortality, and eternal life of man.—Doctrine and Covenants 22:23.

These passages bear record of God's ownership of the earth and man's stewardship over it. Many men have made remarkable progress through the centuries in turning the resources of God's creation to their own use, but they have not always recognized or accepted their stewardship responsibility to God and their fellowmen in sharing that which was intended for all.

For, behold, the beasts of the field, and the fowls of the air, and that which cometh of the earth, is ordained for the use of man, for food, and for raiment, and that he might have in abundance, but it is not given that one man should possess that which is above another.— Doctrine and Covenants 49:3.

While scriptures provide the moral background upon which the principles of stewardship are based, there are other reasons for accepting them as a way of life. The philosophy of stewardship is more comprehensive than the term "doctrine of stewardship." Philosophy is defined as "a critique and analysis of fundamental beliefs as they come to be conceptualized and formulated." This seems to lend itself to broader consideration than that which is implied in doctrine, which is defined as ". . . a creed of principles, presented for acceptance or belief."[1] In either case, stewardship as a way of life may prove stimulating, challenging, and helpful.

The Cause of Zion is both process and goal of the church. As a process it is an ever changing movement both in its conceptual envisioning and its practical implementation. As a goal it calls for restudy and readjustment as each step becomes a reality. But Zion develops only in proportion to the acceptance of stewardship responsibility by an ever increasing number of people who believe in it as leading to a better way of life.

The thinking person who acknowledges God as Creator and owner wants to know how he can best serve. He will ask: "What service is required? What talents and skills are most needed? What is the program of the church?" Sometimes there is no simple answer. However in dealing with such subjects as the gathering, the storehouse, and financial administration I shall cover some of these practical needs.

The call which came to men in the initial organization of the church was in a sense a declaration of purpose, such as the call to Joseph Smith, Jr., who at the time it was received—November 1, 1831—was twenty-six years of age. This revelation (Doctrine and Covenants 1:4) is a reaffirmation of previous calls:

Wherefore I the Lord, knowing the calamity which should come upon the inhabitants of the earth, called upon my servant Joseph Smith, Jr., and spake unto him from heaven, and gave him commandments, and also gave commandments to others, that they should proclaim these things unto the world . . . that the fullness of my gospel might be proclaimed by the weak and the simple, unto the ends of the world, and before kings and rulers.

Other men were called by revelation to positions of trust with specific instructions to "keep my commandments and seek to bring forth and establish the cause of Zion."[2] The opening assertion in each of these revelations is "a great and marvelous work is about to come forth among the children of men."

Other revelations establish certain principles which have to do with man's responsibilities and obligations.

Accountability: "Every man shall be made accountable unto me a steward over his own property, or that which he has received by consecration" (Doctrine and Covenants 42:9b).

Surplus consecrations: "Thou wilt remember the poor, and consecrate of thy properties for their support" (42:8b).

Honesty and labor: "Thou shalt not be idle; for he that is idle shall not eat the bread nor wear the garments of the laborer" (42:12b).

Bases of equality: "Inasmuch as is sufficient for himself and family" (42:9b).

"That every man who has need may be amply supplied, and receive according to his wants" (42:10a).

Good citizenship: "All things shall be made sure according to the laws of the land" (51:1e).

Leadership requirements: "It is not meet that I should command in all things, for he that is compelled in all things, the same is a slothful and not a wise servant. . . .
Men should be anxiously engaged in a good cause and do many things of their own free will, and bring to pass much righteousness; for the power is in them, wherein they are agents unto themselves. . . . But he that doeth not anything until he is commanded, and receiveth a commandment with doubtful heart, and keepeth it with slothfulness, the same is damned" (58:6).

The foregoing excerpts from revelations may be considered as the disciplines of stewardship. They are but a few of the requisites for building a community life wherein men can find opportunity for personal and group development on the basis of Christian fellowship. There are many more which have to do with social structure and organization. These excerpts, as is true with all revelations in the Doctrine and Covenants, have bearing upon each other. The philosophy of stewardship needs to be considered as a whole or in the relationship that each has to the other if its deep significance is to be understood. To some the disciplines may seem too strict, too complex, but when taken as a whole present a philosophy that could well be made viable in the present age. There is a wide gap between what such a philosophy calls for and what prevails. This is evident in the writing of Allen Wheelis who summarizes what has happened in the history of civilization: "The age is ending, the house is coming down—all the rafters, all the towers, all the clocks. It was built of a dream. The dream closes."[3] He recounts the startling scientific discoveries which have resulted in the unveiling of traditions and sometimes myths of religion, and also recognizes the contribution of science to the increase in knowledge which has made truth more apparent. He does not, however, discount the contribution of the church through the Middle Ages and on up and to the present. He tells not only of the contributions of the scientists through this same period but of the mind and soul and prophecy. He writes: "The use of tools is inseparably connected with the development of man, and the master craftsman engaged in his work provides one of the luminous moments of the human spirit."[4]

Of the search for truth he says:

Now, knowing the truth we achieve is changed by the chase and the receiver, we know no pursuit can be pure. It behooves us more urgently, therefore, to consider what we are about, what we may do with the truth we achieve. For if it should come about that what we do is utterly to destroy the world, then from the far side of desolation we would cry out—were anyone left to weep or to reflect—that primitive man who viewed the world with awe and wonder knew it better than we who fathomed the furthermost secrets of the atom. . . . May we see but well enough to lay aside the weapons with which we are about to destroy, along with that little we do see, a potential of the experience we know not of.[5]

While the stewardship philosophy may seem too idealistic most of us do have ideals toward which we try to direct our lives. And some "dreams" do take form with the passing of time. God said through his prophet Joseph Smith, Jr., in the very beginning of the coming forth of his church, ". . . the works, and the designs, and the purposes of God cannot be frustrated, neither can they come to naught, for God doth not walk in crooked paths."[6]

The faith of others of centuries ago regarding a continuity of God's work may give us hope for a better world both now and in the near future. But we cannot help being aware of the weaknesses existing in our present society with its inner-city poverty, unemployment, labor problems, laxity in law enforcement, inadequate school facilities and teaching staff, disillusioned youth, and the lack of established bases of faith in God. In addition to all of this, there is the ever present threat of the expansion of war and the complete annihilation of the human race.

In the past as I have engaged in worship or classwork concerning the building of God's kingdom, I have not been able to separate my concern for the needs of society from the experiences of those particular times or of the present hour. I have found myself under the necessity of reviewing again and again the history of man's relationship to man in light of the revelation of God's will expressed in the Bible, the Book of Mormon, and the Doctrine and Covenants.

Recent authors have called attention more effectively than ever before to some of the values to be found in the history of the Jewish people, whose writings bear evidence of their belief in God and their adherence to the laws of Moses, as well as to the prophetic utterances of the prophets.

Emil Brunner writes of the difference between the Old and New Testaments in relation to social justice:

Although the New Testament contains the outlines of a doctrine of earthly justice, it contains but scant indication of a Christian doctrine of mundane institutions, nor is that in any way surprising. ... The message of Christ and his apostles, and the primitive Christian community, were concerned with greater things than the framing of worldly systems. ... The Christian community at its foundation, since it formed a tiny minority in the Roman Empire, and had no voice in public affairs, the shape of worldly systems was of no immediate interest.—The situation of the first Christians was radically different from that of the Israelites at the time of their national independence.

For this reason the Old Testament presents a totally different picture from the New Testament. Here we find in the state, law and economics systems which are as magnificent as they are unique. Above all, in the Prophets of the Old Testament the demand for justice in the name of God is put forward more urgently than anywhere else in history. For the people of Israel were to be and wished to be the people of God, but the will of their Lord was to be and had to be manifest not only in the personal, inward life of individuals, not only in the life of the community serving God, but also in the public institutions of the people as a whole. . . . The divine revelation in the Old Testament is a preliminary stage of the revelation of Jesus Christ.[7]

Present-day Israel represents a search for social justice as well as a nation for the Jewish people. The Cause of Zion of the Latter Day Saints is that of achieving a society based on the principles of Christianity expressed in the statement of Jesus: "I am come that they might have life, and that they might have it more abundantly."[8]

The records of the Hebrews were supplemented over a century ago by the Book of Mormon. In reviewing one of the most dramatic portions of that remarkable book I found it possible to gather new assurance that we might overcome the hazards of the age in which we live and look forward to the realization of that kingdom envisioned by the prophets of old. This is contained in the Book of Mosiah, particularly chapters 1 to 4, which tell of the reign of King Benjamin beginning with "And now there was no more contention in all the land of Zarahemla, among all the people who belonged to King Benjamin, so that King Benjamin had continual peace all the remainder of his days." (See also the Words of Mormon 1:26-27.)

This covered a period of time when King Banjamin, nearing the close of his reign, decided to turn his kingdom over to his three sons.

And he caused that they should be taught in all the language of his fathers, that thereby they might become men of understanding; and that they might know concerning the prophecies which had been spoken by the mouths of their fathers, which were delivered them by the hand of the Lord.—Mosiah 1:3.

To make this effective he asked his son, Mosiah, to call the inhabitants of his land together that he might make public transfer of his responsibilities and give instruction to his people. In response

the people gathered themselves together throughout all the land, that they might go up to the temple to hear the words which King Benjamin should speak unto them. And there were a great number, even so many that they did not number them; for they had multiplied exceedingly, and waxed great in the land.—Mosiah 1:28, 29.

King Benjamin taught his people their responsibility to God through sacrificial offerings and compliance with scriptural laws. At this particular time they responded, bringing "the firstlings of their flocks" with the intent that "they might give thanks to the Lord their God, . . . who had delivered them out of the hands of their enemies and had appointed just men to be their teachers, and also, a just man to be their king" (Mosiah 1:30, 31).

King Benjamin, one of the truly great leaders of all time, was humble and filled with a sincere desire to serve his God and his people. In his address he reminded them of the fact that he had asked neither for "gold nor silver, nor any manner of riches" nor would he allow them to make slaves of one another or permit them to "commit any manner of wickedness." Finally he reminded them:

And even I, myself, have labored with mine own hands, that I might serve you, and that ye should not be laden with taxes, and that there should nothing come upon you which was grievous to be borne; and of all these things which I have spoken, ye yourselves are witnesses this day.—Mosiah 1:46.

He appealed to them to serve God unselfishly and lovingly, saying that to do so was a great privilege. "And

behold, all that he requires of you, is to keep his commandments; and he has promised you that if ye would keep his
commandments, ye should prosper in the land" (Mosiah
1:55).

He also reminded them of the needs of others:

I would that ye should impart of your substance to the poor, every
man according to that which he hath, such as feeding the hungry,
clothing the naked, visiting the sick, and administering to their relief,
both spiritually and temporally, according to their wants.—Mosiah
2:43.

Having approached the subject of stewardship as a
philosophy and considered some of the disciplines essential in
the application of the principles, I shall take note of some
further evaluation of the objectives before us. The prime
purpose has been designated as seeking "to bring forth and
establish the cause of Zion" through stewardship.

The term steward has been used in past centuries to
describe the managing of property.

Emil Brunner in his book *Justice and the Social Order*
writes:

Strictly speaking, all ownership of things is "acquired," for nobody
is born with it. The most natural kind of property is that earned by
work, since it is most closely bound up with the person. What a man
has earned belongs to him; he has a right to it. But from the standpoint
of the order of creation, a further principle holds good: Even this
property which belongs to him does not belong to him unconditionally,
since it is held under God. With respect to other men, man is an owner,
he has plenary control over what belongs to him. With respect to God
he is always a steward, a man with an account to render. He is obliged
not by justice but by compassion to give to those in need out of what is
entirely his property, but those in need have no right to it. It is,
however, true that all property from the standpoint of justice, is held
subject to the reservation of fellowship. For all property is acquired
under conditions which the acquirer has not himself created. . . .[9]

These "conditions" to which he refers are the state and

community, which tend to increase value with increase in population and improvements made possible through taxes.

Webster defines a steward as a "household officer on a lord's estate, having charge of the cattle; later a manager in the administration of a manor or estate; also one who actively directs affairs, a manager. . . ."

Definitions clearly indicate that a steward has the responsibility of management. In latter-day revelation, as already pointed out, stewardship as a principle takes on broader meaning and has become a significant part of our religious philosophy. It is, in fact, basic to any approach we wish to make—to the solution of problems which we face both personally and as a nation.

Because stewardship is basic to individual happiness and ultimately to the peace of the world, I wish to discuss certain elements of it and try to make some application that will have practical value for all of us. First we should take inventory of those things which are God-given.

I mention, first of all, that animating force within us which makes us what we are. Our spirit, mind, and body are all God-given.

Next, we are given a dwelling place, a home. It may be richly furnished or lacking many of the basic necessities that make for comfort, but it is a place in which to dwell.

In addition to the aforementioned we have businesses, professions, trades, or crafts. We have clothing, furniture, automobiles, machinery, and hundreds of items over which we must exercise stewardship responsibility.

The manner in which we use physical things is a matter of the *mind.* The choice we make is an expression of our God-given agency.

The Lord said unto Enoch, Behold these your brethren; they are the workmanship of my own hands, and I gave unto them their knowledge, in the day I created them; and in the garden of Eden gave I unto man his agency.—Doctrine and Covenants 36:7a, b.

From this responsibility of stewardship there is no escape. We face it every day. What we do with our God-given intellect and material resources determines not only the course of our lives but the course of the world. Our future depends on our right of agency in making choices in harmony with the divine Will.

Our understanding of our relationship with God can be enhanced by a careful reading of this scripture:

Man was also in the beginning with God. Intelligence, or the light of truth, was not created or made, neither indeed can be. All truth is independent in that sphere in which God has placed it, to act for itself, as all intelligence also, otherwise there is no existence.

Behold, here is the agency of man, and here is the condemnation of man, because that which was from the beginning is plainly manifest unto them, and they receive not the light. And every man whose spirit receiveth not the light is under condemnation, for man is spirit. The elements are eternal, and spirit and element, inseparably connected, receiveth a fullness of joy. . . .

The glory of God is intelligence, or, in other words, light and truth.—Doctrine and Covenants 90:5, 6.

Thus we see that we have our beginning with God, and only through the wrong exercise of agency do we depart from him. Our stewardship, therefore, is to be thought of not just in terms of the moment but in terms of those purposes which are eternal, for our spirits are immortal.

Let us think for the moment of what we can do with our God-given intellect. What use do we make of our minds in our daily activities. What do we fill them with? I say "fill" because they are repositories where the impressions of what we see or hear or experience are recorded. As stewards we have the responsibility of segregating and determining, to a large extent, that which we retain to help us meet whatever

140

issues and problems may confront us. It is important, therefore, that we carefully evaluate the material we deposit there.

As we review man's progress, we must conclude that there never has been and probably never will be any cataclysmic change which will catapult humanity toward the worthwhile goals of life. The Industrial Revolution and the scientific-technological-social revolution now in process probably come nearer to doing this than all other movements of economic character in human history. But these have not brought spiritual, ethical, and moral results to match the material benefits which have accrued to portions of the world population.

We need to examine our belief relative to the principles of stewardship to see if it will stand the test in relation to meeting human need today. We must also appraise the extent to which that belief is expressed by members of the church.

In doing so it is essential to establish the basis of the law which should govern us and then examine certain goals and standards which are before us for achievement. The principle of the accounting requires our primary attention:

> For it is expedient that I, the Lord, should make every man accountable, as stewards over earthly blessings, which I have made and prepared for my creatures.
>
> I, the Lord, stretched out the heavens, and builded the earth as a very handy work; and all things therein are mine; and it is my purpose to provide for my saints, for all things are mine; but it must needs be done in mine own way—Doctrine and Covenants 101:2c, d.

The real point of beginning in making an accounting is developing a proper attitude. Some may question that God is the Creator and Owner of all. I accept this as a fundamental truth. Accounting is essential in the stewardship of time as well as temporal wealth. God has said that we are to render an account of our stewardship both in time and in eternity. We are accountable not only to him but to the church and to our fellowmen. The basis on which we build during our stay on earth charts the course of our eternal life.

The use of time has a marked bearing upon the developmnt of our minds, while our exercise of agency (mind) determines to a large extent the use of time. We have then as our responsibility as stewards the use of mind and the use of time. Let us now briefly consider our stewardship over material resources.

We live in an economy which is commercially organized. Just as there is a struggle for control for the minds of men, so is there a struggle for the control of physical resources. The ships of America traverse every known seaway and encircle the globe. The formation of capital in corporations and trusts makes possible the expansion of industry and business until its effect is felt upon almost every living soul, from the impoverished millions in India to the industrial capitalists of America. What is true in this respect regarding America is also true regarding other great nations. The expansion of the common market in Europe, the outreach of American business capital in nations abroad, and foreign capital invested in new business ventures in America create competition which affects the individual at home or abroad. Everything we touch, see, acquire, and use (or waste) has something to do with our personal stewardship and our stewardship as a nation.

With a sense of our responsibility as stewards, let us ask ourselves the direction we wish to go. Do we want to retain the God-given agency which is ours? Do we wish to separate ourselves from God in following courses not in harmony with his will? Do we wish to subordinate ourselves to the domination of a dictatorial government? Do we want to retain the freedom we have inherited from the founders of our country? In answering these, we need to consider other questions which relate to our church, our doctrine, and our philosophy.

We talk much about Zion. We discuss Zionic principles, community building, and related subjects. The establishment of Zion depends on what we decide to do about it. The acceptance of stewardship responsibility imposes upon us certain choices. Fundamentally these are matters of will—that faculty of the mind which determines the use of intellect and physical resources for the attainment of specific ends.

First we need to examine our attitude toward material possessions. Is the listing of them in an inventory or financial statement too much of a task when we consider its importance in keeping accurate records? These are essential for reporting to the government, as well as to the church. It is always rewarding to turn the searchlight inward.

The appraisal of our loyalty and the measurement of our devotion to the ideals which motivate us to serve others are helpful in making the required accounting. They may also be instrumental in developing a pattern of life which, in the normal course of our experience, can result in the proper use of our resources and God-given talents. To the extent that men so develop they can engage in creative undertakings in the fields of stewardship and social progress.

Attitude determines the direction men go and reflects the code of ethics by which they live. Former Secretary of Commerce Luther Hodges, in *The Business Conscience,* wrote:

We cannot see, hear, smell, taste, or touch one of our most personal possessions—our individual code of ethics. Yet our code is an inseparable part of us, and it can be a priceless asset or have less value than a lead nickel; the worth of a personal code will vary from individual to individual.—Page 73.

We are not limited to scripture in establishing a code of ethics which is to govern our conduct, but latter-day scriptures add new light and give purpose to the traditional heritage which has come down through the centuries of time. We should examine—and accept—the principles in which we find both revealed and tested truth.

Basic to all stewardship is the need for clearly defined purpose for individual and family. It is not always a simple matter to establish a life purpose. For today's young person, vocational choices are many and varied. Sometimes years are consumed in finding the best profession. At times in the past this was not true; opportunities were limited. Apprenticeships were the usual avenue open to craftsmen, and often children followed in their parents' trade, business, or vocation.

The present educational system provides a much broader field for training in the arts, sciences, business, and professions. John W. Gardner, in his book, *Excellence,* refers to the change which has taken place in our society.

The vestiges of stratification will exist, but the great drama of American education has been the democratization of educational opportunity over the past century. This has been one of the great social revolutions.—Page 41.

He points out something of the scope of education for the future:

It is possible to have excellence in education and at the same time to seek to educate everyone to the limit of his ability. A society such as ours has no choice but to seek the development of human potentialities at all levels.—Page 77.

But he also points out the need for a balanced college program:

Properly understood, the college or university is the instrument of one kind or another of further education of those whose capacities fit them for that kind of an education. It should not be regarded as the sole means of establishing one's human worth. It should not be seen as the unique key to happiness, self-respect, and inner confidence.—Pages 80-81.

The purpose of the application of stewardship principles is not one of taking from but adding to both temporal and spiritual values in the lives of men everywhere to help bring about a more equitable sharing of the good things of God's creation, to develop a people who ultimately could live in peace and Christian fellowship. H. G. Wells supports this in his *Outline of History*. He attributes the development of the idea of one God and the free conscience of mankind to the Hebrew prophets:

From their time onward there was to be found in human thought the idea of one rule in the world and of a promise and possibility of active and splendid peace and happiness in human affairs. . . .

Then Jesus founded the universal religion of Christianity; also the prophet Mohammed appeared in Arabia and founded Islam. . . . 2400 years ago and six to eight thousand years after the walls of the first Sumerian cities arose the ideas of a moral unity of mankind and world peace came into the world.—Volume 1, page 217.

Today the principles of stewardship are accepted and are being put in practice by many denominations to various degrees throughout the world. In many instances we have been invited to share that which we have with them and they, in turn, have shared their experience and practical achievements with us. We are learning that social progress in the fullest sense depends on members of society complying with the divine principles of life. While we are considering the Zionic society in the specific sense, the same principles apply to the larger society of which we are a part.

Today billions of dollars are being spent for armaments. Additional billions are being spent to strengthen the economic foundations of underprivileged countries. Billions are also being spent for liquor, tobacco, and other nonessential items, while millions of people lack the basic necessities of life. Although some see the solution to these problems in the "isms" being promulgated, as a church we often express the thought that the remedy is to be found in the application of the principles of stewardship. To this end we should probe our minds and reevaluate our talents and resources.

What does this probing reveal to us? Is our present status of achievement one which satisfies? Have we used our monetary resources wisely? Have we applied our talents to productive use? How do we measure up when we review our record of tithing paid, offerings given, and surplus contributed?

What does this probing reveal in respect to our use of time? Are we informed as to the basic requirements of stewardship? Have we spent a reasonable time in study and research? Have we been faithful in church attendance? Have we used our time wisely in improving our economic status? Have we considered the needs of others, visited the sick, and remembered the lonely, the friendless, the destitute? Have we taken reasonable time for recreation and meditation in seeking release from daily pressures? Have we eaten and exercised properly to conserve our health?

What does this probing reveal to us about the use of talents? How much effort do we put forth in their development? Have we learned what we are most qualified to do? What are our abilities in the arts, music, speech, drama? What are our avocations? What is our productive potential in the professions, trades, business, industry?

Does all that we seek to do reflect the depth of our desire to establish Zion?

If we approach this matter prayerfully, we shall be inspired to give greater service, improve our church attendance, and contribute more in tithes and offerings. In the church administrative procedures will be tempered by consideration for the welfare and happiness of all, and physical, economic, and spiritual blessings will accrue—because this is the basic purpose of stewardship.

> ... Whatever ye do according to the will of the Lord, is the Lord's business. . . . Wherefore be not weary in well-doing, for ye are laying the foundation of a great work. And out of small things proceedeth that which is great. . . . For, behold, I say unto you that Zion shall flourish, and the glory of the Lord shall be upon her, and she shall be an ensign unto the people, and there shall come unto her out of every nation under heaven.—Doctrine and Covenants 64:6b, c; 8a.

Throughout my many years of membership in the church the principle of stewardship has been a point of reference on which I based most of the major decisions it has been my responsibility to make. The question arose early in my life as to how I could best fulfill whatever mission might be mine. In these days the problem of identity is for many a perplexing one. This can be solved in the fullest sense only when one recognizes a relationship to God. Moses was faced with this when he was commissioned to "bring forth the children of Israel out of Egypt." He responded by asking, "Who am I, that I should go unto Pharaoh, and that I should bring forth the children of Israel out of Egypt?" In the dialogue which ensued Moses found his identity with God. And so it is with all men when they seek to fulfill their eternal purpose.

Stewardship means many things to many people, depending on their background, culture, environment, education, experience, intellectual capacity, religious beliefs, and inherent gifts. Despite this, there is much that all have in common. A growing sensitivity to the basic rights of others can emerge from the application of the principle that God created all men of one blood and that there is enough in his

147

physical creation to supply their needs. The great task is to perfect the process of distributing resources according to the need. This is the primary object of stewardship, but underlying all such endeavor is that of developing Christlike personalities and efficient stewards in all areas of life.

In the almost century and a half since the coming forth of the Restoration these principles have been taught from pulpit, in the classroom, and at home. I doubt that there has ever been a time in history when their worth has been more obvious than today when the world continues to face crisis upon crisis. Moral fiber is under terrific strain, and there is need for leadership inspired of God.

No nation is exempt from the consequences of social and political unrest. This ranges from minority groups seeking to find their rightful place in society to small "underprivileged" nations struggling for identity.

The Zionic principles which motivate us in the United States, and especially in the Center Place, are more challenging now than in all our past experience. The commission ". . . and this gospel shall be preached unto every nation, kindred, tongue, and people" requires personnel trained in languages and professionally equipped to provide maximum service and ministry.

At its inception the Restoration philosophy was not one of doing without, nor is it at the present, but it does call for self-discipline in the management of time, talents, and resources. It also requires that the individual's goals be related to the goals of the church, not geared to personal satisfaction alone. Jesus said, "He who seeketh to save his life shall lose it; and he who loseth his life for my sake shall find it" (Matthew 10:34).

If as a church we have failed to accomplish what we should have in the past, the present still provides an opportunity for us to fulfill our mission. This will not be easily or quickly realized. We must think of it in terms of decades, and the important decade is the one which we are now beginning—today, this week, this month. It is important because our world will move in one of two directions—either a continuation of war, acceleration of economic problems including debt, and laxity in the administration of justice or a change to an aroused and informed public that supports faith in God and in the right of men to develop with the courage of convictions based on an integrity of life which places the welfare of others above self. Paternal care of citizens by government has place in certain areas where the individual cannot provide his needs, but government can also invade the privacy of our homes if we are not careful. Education regarding individual responsibility is essential.

The approach that our church makes to this problem is through its program of stewardship. There are many references containing information on stewardship, including the following:

The Priesthood Journals, Volumes 1-9; *The Priesthood Manual,* 1964, 1972; *Priesthood Orientation Studies,* 1964; *Restoration Stewardship Guidelines (In the Manner Designed of God,* by the Presiding Bishopric contains references).

---

1. *The American Heritage Dictionary of the English Language.*
2. Oliver Cowdery (Doctrine and Covenants 6:3a), Hyrum Smith (10:3a), Joseph Knight, Sr. (11:3b), David Whitmer (12:3a).
3. *The End of the Modern Age,* page 3, Basic Books, Inc., Publishers, New York and London.
4. *Ibid.,* page 92.
5. *Ibid.,* pages 112, 115.
6. Doctrine and Covenants 2:1.
7. Emil Brunner, *Justice and the Social Order,* Harper, New York and London, 1945, pages 118-119.
8. John 10:10.
9. *Justice and the Social Order,* page 149.

Chapter 7

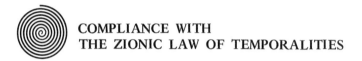

COMPLIANCE WITH
THE ZIONIC LAW OF TEMPORALITIES

Awake, awake, put on thy strength, O Zion; put on thy beautiful garments O Jerusalem, the holy city; . . . and then shall they say, How beautiful upon the mountains are the feet of him that bringeth good tidings unto them, that publisheth peace; that bringeth good tidings unto them of good, that publisheth salvation; that saith unto Zion, Thy God reigneth!—Isaiah 52:1, 7, I.V.

Wherefore, verily I say unto you, that all things unto me are spiritual, and not at any time have I given unto you a law which was temporal, neither any man, nor the children of men; neither Adam your father, whom I created; behold, I gave unto him that he should be an agent unto himself.—Doctrine and Covenants 28:9a, b.

During the years it has been my privilege to serve as a minister of Jesus Christ, particularly as Presiding Bishop, I have had varied experiences in respect to teaching the principles of the temporal law and in administering the temporal affairs of the church. At the Lamoni Reunion in 1943 I preached a sermon which was recorded in shorthand by a member of the church, transcribed, and a copy sent to me. I am including here those portions of the sermon which verified some promises pertaining to the growth of the church which have occurred since that time.

When I am faced with difficulties and problems that seem too great for me to resolve I find that there are two courses open to me. One is to face them alone; the other is to seek the inspiration of Almighty God.

Sometimes perhaps both ways are blended as one. Often I am also strengthened by association with my brethren and by the knowledge that truth is contained in the scriptures. If I were to select a pertinent text it would be the promise found in Doctrine and Covenants 2:1: "The works and the designs, and the purposes of God cannot be frustrated, neither can they come to naught. . . ."

I would associate with this text one found in the Book of Mormon, written by Moroni at a time when those with whom he had been associated had been killed and all must have appeared to him to have been lost: "For the eternal purposes of the Lord shall roll on until all his promises are fulfilled."[1] In such scripture I find the basis of a radiant hope.

I have been concerned as I have occupied my position of responsibility that there might be those who would think I could not rejoice in this role. Many times my burden has been heavy, but I can testify that I have attempted to build my life on the hope of the gospel of Jesus Christ, which, in essence, is that together we can enjoy a more abundant life by participating collectively in the work to which we have been called—the establishment of God's kingdom here on the earth. And if at any time I register concern it is not because I lack faith but because I am anxious to implement the social order that I envisioned even as a small boy which could mark the dawning of a new world and the return of Jesus Christ. Because I have seen so clearly the happiness and glory that can result when we work together toward this end, I have accepted the responsibility to do the job that our Lord and Savior wants done.

Like many of you I came to Lamoni filled with hope. I left a community that meant a great deal to me to come here and assume a responsibility in this stake. In so doing I asked one question: "What does the church want me to do?" I was instructed to do what I could to bring about an organization of the economic life of our people in this stake that together we might build the kingdom. What a challenge! What an opportunity! So I moved forward in the hope that together we might lay some foundations. I remained in this position only temporarily, however, then was called on to responsibilities that I felt were too difficult for me to face.

I remember, when I left this community, that I sought the counsel of Brother Garver. We drove around the streets of Kansas City three or four hours one night discussing the problems of the church. When I asked him whether I should assume this responsibility to become a member of the Presiding Bishopric or turn from it, he merely said that it was my responsibility to make the decision. On another occasion when I asked his advice we thought through the problem together. Out of those experiences I learned something—that individuals who assume responsibility must make their own decisions, but that through brotherly guidance they may be helped to arrive at a proper decision.

Basically there is just one goal ahead of this church—the building of a social order wherein the divine will may be expressed. Other goals are but intermediate steps toward this.

I recall one occasion when we thought that we had more or less gotten our feet on the ground the order for the closing of the banks came. The money which we had deposited to give assistance to our missionary families, to satisfy the creditors of the church, to put a roof on the new hospital that was then in only a partially constructed state was suddenly gone. Left without a dollar in the bank, we had to start all over again. Many members asked, "What shall we do?" There was only one answer . . . "Go on." We had a moral obligation to those who gave their lives that this Restoration movement might come into existence. We had responsibilities to the Saints down through the years since the Restoration had been effected. We had responsibilities to our children for whom we yet hoped to build a society wherein they could find peace and happiness. So in spite of discouraging experiences, we have continued to move forward in faith that the day of salvation will come . . . and we have been making progress.

As the church emerged from an almost bankrupt condition we moved forward in faith, irrespective of obstacles. Today we can in retrospect chart the year-by-year course of our emergence from that near catastrophe to a reasonably substantial financial position. There are those now who would ask, "Is it not time now to relax?" Looking to the years just ahead relative to the financial administration of the church and the economic problems which face us, I can say that we must redouble our efforts if we are to speed up the business of building the kingdom.

There are those who think that we have lost sight of some of the major issues confronting the church. There are others who would bring about the establishment of the kingdom with a wave of the hand. Still others would have us launch into projects which we are not yet prepared to execute in harmony with the divine will. If we go back in our experience and review what we have accomplished we shall find that it is not because any one of us individually has sought to bring about the present condition; rather it is because we complied with basic laws of the church and this resulted in freedom from financial worries. We shall not deviate from this law which contains the social philosophy of this church. We have yet, however, to implement the part pertaining to reserves.

How shall we establish the kingdom? Through compliance with the divine law. Ever since I can remember we have been a struggling people. Is this in harmony with divine law? As a boy I often heard that the gospel was for the poor, but those who said that ignored the fact that the law of the church makes broad provision for meeting the needs of many people. Included in it is the plan for a storehouse organization through which financial resources may be distributed to meet the needs of a society. This will provide for the poor, for the selection of people with skills and abilities, for the elimination of debt, and for other basic organizational needs essential to the gathering. The law calls for the consecration of surplus.

The day is near at hand when this church shall move out under the influence of Almighty God and call for the consecration of our surplus. But what shall we do in the meantime? We must build a financial structure that will not only give assurance to the members of the church but evidence to the world that we mean what we are talking about. Hopefully not many more years will pass before the call shall come for a consecration of surpluses. We are now out of debt . . . out of bondage. For the first six months of 1943 we have not only paid all of the expenses of the church but accumulated $228,000 in surpluses. If during the balance of this year we can continue on the same level, we will have set aside reserves in the amount of $500,000. We say that this year and next year it is within the range of possibility of this church not only to meet its operating expenses, but to set up almost a million dollars of reserves. Now I am not placing confidence in the dollar. My trust is that through compliance with the law that has been given to us we can begin the effective functioning of the storehouse. We can add men to our missionary list, and they can go out with authority because the church is evidencing its belief in its doctrine. As we move forward with faith in God and work cooperatively with one another, then surely we shall receive the endowment of God's Holy Spirit, This added to the intelligence should enable us to bring confidence to a world in distress.

May we become ever more conscious of our responsibility to give

153

everything we have in the way of talents, resources, and devotion to the cause in which we are engaged. When we do this there shall radiate from us a hope that will attract others to the church. I look forward with faith to the future and pledge to do whatever is within my power to hasten the building of God's kingdom.

Going back to some of the underlying factors and developments that helped to form the foundation for this 1943 sermon I suggest that we look briefly at the decade of the 1920's.

The famous new-era bull market, which began in 1921, reached a dizzy peak in 1929, terminated in collapse in 1932 (June), represented a cycle which in both duration and magnitude exceeded by far every major price movement in the 1871-1949 span, a mass speculation orgy without any special foundation in economic or political developments. (In this case, however, the speculation produced portentous economic and political results.)—*Security Analysis,* page 23, Graham-Dodd-Cottle (fourth edition), McGraw Hill, New York.

The boom and the collapse proved almost disastrous to the church. The following excerpts from an editorial by President Frederick M. Smith is indicative of the deep feeling of members regarding that period:

So today the troubled conditions, the prevalence of working factors difficult to judge, the collapse of some institutions, conventions, and customs which have long prevailed, the uncertainties which have quite suddenly crept into social conditions, all present a group of factors which enter into our forward looking today, which gives to the present New Year's season a setting quite its own. . . .

We must not forget that with the warnings from Divinity have come instructions of preparation for the coming of unfavorable times. We should be greatly concerned about measuring our progress along the lines of instruction given. Are we prepared against the day of overturning which has been suggested in the conditions prevailing? I fear we have been dilatory.—*Saints' Herald,* Volume 77, December 24, 1930.

The opening of the 1930 Centennial World Conference of

the church had been looked forward to as a milestone of progress for the church:

We have been saying "Forward to 1930 and beyond!" 1930 is here. We here and now celebrate a century of endeavor. A few short days, and weeks, and months, and this time of observance shall have passed. Then to the *beyond!*—L.E.F., *Saints' Herald,* Volume 77, April 9, 1930, page 418.

The following was published in the *Herald* of December 24, 1930:

The increase in general church revenue from tithes and offerings, received up to Saturday, December 20, has enabled us to release three months' allowance checks due missionaries' families. As fast as additional funds are received, more checks will be sent. Other definite arrangements have been made to pay current bills, obligations, and interest charges due January 1.—Signed First Presidency, F. M. Smith; Presiding Bishopric, Albert Carmichael.

Some years ago we developed a chart titled "Increase or Deficit of General Fund Income over Expense for Period 1921 to Date," which was kept current throughout the years. I shall limit my comments on it to include only the years 1921 to 1965 inclusive as my term of office as Presiding Bishop terminated at the 1966 World Conference. In the 1921-1930 period inclusive, the church operated on a deficit basis seven years. From 1931 up to the present time with the exception of 1933 (when adjustments to reduce the budget could not be made fast enough to meet declining income) the church has operated with a substantial net increase. From this increase appropriations have been made to Auditorium construction, Independence Sanitarium and Hospital construction, Graceland College buildings, Operating Reserve Fund, Missionary Reserve Fund, Ministerial Reserve Fund,*

---

*Ministerial Reserve Fund has been increased from current appropriations since 1946.

House of Worship Fund, Houses of Worship Revolving Fund, and miscellaneous expenditures.

It is to the genesis of this change of administration and fiscal policy that I wish to direct attention. In 1943 we could look back upon the years of rigid adherence with some degree of assurance that the change in policy was not only necessary at the time it was adopted but also essential to the future growth and fiscal stability of the church.

In the last quarter of 1930 some of us in the Order of Bishops as well as other members of the Board of Appropriations expressed our deep concern about our church financial situation. The matter was given attention by the Board of Appropriations which was to have met in December 1930 (postponed until February 12, 1931).[2]

Previously a committee on which I served was appointed to make an analysis of the financial situation of the church. It was a discouraging task. Church Auditor Amos Allen and I spent hours every day from the time we were appointed until the date of our report keeping in touch with all members of the committee.

At the Board of Appropriations meeting held February 13 changes were made in personnel of the Presiding Bishopric; these were covered in a document dated February 11, 1931, and signed by Frederick M. Smith. Bishops M. H. Siegfried and J. A. Becker resigned, and Bishop Albert Carmichael continued as Presiding Bishop until the Conference of 1932. Bishop J. A. Becker continued to serve in the Bishop's office for several years and rendered valuable service to the Presiding Bishopric. L. F. P. Curry succeeded Bishop Carmichael as Presiding Bishop, and I was his counselor. Bishop Becker also served as president of the Central Development Company (a church real estate holding corporation) until January 31, 1961.

Preparing the budget for 1931 was a major task. In an article titled "The Revised Budget," L. F. P. Curry noted the following:

An expense budget was approved by the Board of Appropriations February 12. Comparative figures total

1930	$716,462.57
1931	393,430.00

It was noted further, that the cash income for 1930 was $426,000.00; the budget for 1931 being $394,000, leaves for debt reduction $32,000.00. Attention was also called to the fact that total interest requirements listed in the budget amounted to $80,500.00.[3]

In the report submitted by the analysis committee it was noted that the current liabilities to be paid in 1931 amounted to over $337,000, included in which was an item of over $52,000 of appointee family allowances in arrears. To offset these were assets of $152,000. It was noted that the ratio of current liabilities to current assets was 2:1 whereas to be financially sound this ratio should have been 1:2. It was noted also that a payment of $25,000 on General Church bonds would be due July 2, 1932, and this was only a part of the total issue of such bonds, the bulk of which would become due in January 1936. This was not the issue of bonds against the Auditorium in amount of $320,000 yet to be paid. These figures were but a part of the total obligations that would have to be met in the years ahead. Briefly stated the church had obligations totaling $1,866,000.

Bishop Curry and I spent many hours together studying the problem, working out a debt payment program, writing articles, visiting the Saints wherever and whenever we could. The debt payment program was approved by the General Conference of 1932. The First Presidency and Council of Twelve gave unanimous support and gave excellent leadership in stake, district, and field organization.

It was a difficult responsibility to have to release men

from the mission field, close down various departments, and lay off personnel who had been deeply committed to serving the church. Nor was the reduction in costs limited to the General Church. The same policy applied to Graceland College, Herald Publishing House, the Sanitarium and Hospital, homes for the aged, and every area of administrative services.

In view of the fact that we felt the whole program of debt reduction should be in keeping with the basic principles contained in the law of temporalities, I am quoting the content of a talk I made at Lamoni, Iowa, on December 28, 1931:

A careful analysis of the revelations received by the church up to the time of the death of the Martyr reveals that the purpose of the Restoration in a large part, if not in whole, is to set forth the relationship of men to their material possessions and to one another. Practically one third of the revelations received have to do with the establishment of Zion, bearing particularly on the subject of property rights through the process of stewardships, inheritances, and the gathering.

In Doctrine and Covenants 59:4 and 101:2 the Lord states that material things were created for man. As Latter Day Saints we have looked forward to the time when through the processes previously mentioned the purpose of the Restoration might be achieved. Today, instead of being in the position of leadership that God intended his church should assume, we find ourselves in as deep an economic morass as the rest of the world.

Perhaps this is due largely to the fact that we have fastened our eyes on the promises held out while giving scant heed to the admonitions which have accompanied them. Paragraph 5 of Section 59 states: "And it pleaseth God that he hath given all these things unto man; for unto this end were they made, *to be used with judgment, not to excess, neither by extortion.*"

It is well that we now give consideration to the meaning of the admonition, and as it has to do with the utilization of material things we should carefully study the factors bearing on the financial law. Such a study requires time, but we have reached a point in our experience when it appears best to "make haste slowly," in order that we might examine our immediate problem in the light of the more distant but greater objective—the establishment of Zion.

Zion involves a myriad of problems most of which are yet unsolved, but our efforts thus far have brought reward in the knowledge that there is a definite relationship between material possessions and spiritual growth. Our present predicament has brought this most forcibly to our attention. If we have learned that progress can be made only as individuals comply with natural, spiritual, and economic laws, we have at least arrived at a point of beginning.

It is said that sacrifice brings spiritual growth. There is always a reward for sacrifice, but also there is always a cost and it is just as imperative that the cost as well as the reward be considered.

Many plans have been suggested for paying off the church debt—all of them with some merit—but for the most part they have been approached on a mathematical basis without giving consideration to the ultimate result. It is important that any plan adopted will not bring about the impoverishment of the membership but will assure security in the future. The plan to be adopted for debt reduction must strengthen both spiritually and financially the individual members, for the church can never be any stronger than its membership and hope to succeed.

The financial policy adopted by the council in 1931 is economically sound and will apply to both church and individual. It was set forth as follows:

1. Arresting expansion (building only as cash is available or other resources justify)
2. Stopping leaks (guarding carefully against unnecessary or unwise expenditures)
3. Liquidating assets (turning into cash all assets not needed for the major purposes of the church: preaching the gospel and building Zion)
4. Balancing the budget (keeping expenses within income)
5. Paying the debt
6. Creating reserves (for the purpose of providing for missionaries during old age or incapacity—also providing for an operating reserve)

If it is sound for the church to arrest expansion when it does not have cash in hand with which to build, it is also sound for the church members.

159

If there are leaks in financial administration by the church it is possible that there are unjustified expenses in the homes of the members.

If the church has unneeded assets which ought to be liquidated, it is possible that individuals have also.

If it is good business for the church to spend no more than it receives, it is good business for the members.

If it is wise for the church to get out of debt, it is for the members.

If safety for the church lies in the creation of reserves members will also benefit from personal reserves.

According to the financial law of the church every man who is physically and mentally able should have the opportunity to support himself and his family and also purchase an inheritance.

In our desire to rid ourselves of debt we must keep in mind that as "there is no shortcut to salvation" neither is there a shortcut to economic freedom. Since we do not believe that deathbed repentance insures immediate entrance to the celestial kingdom, we surely ought not to expect the economic law to be more elastic than the spiritual law.

It is well that we attempt to clarify our thinking in regard to inheritances and stewardships and work in harmony with the principles involved.

There are two major considerations which have a direct bearing on our immediate problem:

1. The financial strength of our membership is sufficient to justify a short-time debt reduction program.
2. The confidence of the members in the ability and intent of the General Church officers is such that they will give support to a program of debt reduction.

The time has come when we must not only know the financial strength of our membership but as a church we must

1. Show our interest by displaying a desire to conserve the resources of the members.
2. Make some approach to the labor problem, providing opportunity for those who are without work.
3. Consider anew "needs and just wants" as related to the members and their responsibility to the church. (This involves reaffirmation on their part that the financial statement is the accounting required.)

4. Reemphasize the basic law in regard to the gathering, stewardships, and inheritances.

Confidence on the part of members can be established only through

1. An educational program which will constantly keep before them the problem as well as marks of progress of the church.
2. An educated priesthood and a printed organ which will reach the membership.

It is quite apparent that we do not have an educated priesthood. General information indicates that not more than 60 percent are active, and it is difficult to establish what percentage know how to function in the office to which they are called. Priesthood members must be educated not in the sense of scholastic standing, although that is helpful, but educated in their church duties.

A program is needed which will get the *Herald* into the homes of at least 60 percent of the members. This in itself is a great task, but a successful program of debt reduction demands that it be given consideration.

These and other problems are to be considered as we move forward, and as we proceed may we do so "with judgment."

The preceding will, I hope, reveal something of the urgency we felt in approaching the task before us in 1931, as well as our concern that we should not lose sight of the basic purpose in our doing so. We knew that we must pay our debts so our creditors would not lose their confidence in us. The payment of the debt *was* accomplished. I wrote of this in 1943 (*Saints' Herald,* March 6, 1943, page 293):

We emphasized the necessity of making 1942 a year of endeavor to eliminate every dollar of debt owed by the church and its institutions. Our World Conference saw fit to approve; and not only did the church give approval to the effort that was being put forth, but the church as a whole in responding to that call as a result of General Conference action, contributed dollar upon dollar until, at the end of December, we had the largest contribution of tithes and offerings in the history of our church; and every dollar of debt of the church and her institutions has been cleared. We face this new year with freedom from debt and with a reasonable cash margin in hand with which to commence the operations of 1943. . . .

There was the one period, however, to which I have previously made brief reference, when hopes dimmed. This was the "Bank Holiday," when the run on banks made it necessary to provide temporary protection for some. Many reopened. Among those that did not was the Jackson County Bank in which the church had funds. In an editorial (*Saints' Herald,* March 8, 1938, page 291) President F. M. Smith described conditions:

When we (Brother DeLapp and I) went into the main room of the bank,* the place was thronged with people. Every officer had a small group of persons about him "talking things over"; every clerk and employee was busy, to the last man. On the faces of all employees and officers were looks of care and concern, and the same look could be seen on the faces of many, if not all, of the patrons. But there was no excitement, no loud talking. On the faces of many could be seen the question, "I wonder what's coming next?" The usual optimism seemed to prevail. "It will be all right soon."

From the news in the press since Friday it seems probable that whatever has been transpiring in banking circles in Kansas City has been happening in most if not all of the states of America, so banking holidays are in vogue. These are "signs of the times." They indicate again how delicate is the balance between confidence and distrust. They indicate again to us as a people how essential it is for us to be organized socially on a basis where Christian charity can displace selfish greed, and where fraternal sympathy and desire to help—rather than self-interest—can become the social and industrial dynamic and provide the motivation for the social contribution.

Later perhaps our financial department will tell us more particularly how the financial situation affects us. In the meantime, we must carry on and remember that we long have been warned against the coming of just such times, so it is not for us to have fear of functioning to the failing of our hearts, but rather it is for us to face the situation with the faith and trust that casts out all fear and in this spirit take up

---

*The Fidelity National Bank and Trust Company, Kansas City, Missouri

anew our task of establishing Zion, for still the cry is, "Onward to Zion."

The response of the Saints to the situation was excellent. I think this is best illustrated by the attitude of one of our fine members who had loaned the church a substantial sum of money. He said, "Brother DeLapp, I am most embarrassed, but I have all my money loaned to the church, or in the Jackson County Bank, and I don't have money to buy groceries for my family. I don't want to trouble you, but if you could let me have a little money I would be very grateful, and if you can't there will be no hard feelings; I'll understand." I answered, "You shouldn't be embarrassed; I am the one who should be. If I could let you have fifty dollars tomorrow, would that do? I'll give you the first that comes in." I did, and this evidence of his love for the church made me feel spiritually enriched. I knew he was representative of many members and with such people we would succeed.

Related Goals, the Auditorium

Although the goals to be reached have seemed far distant at times, there are certain highlights I like to recall. One such is the Auditorium.

I wrote an article in 1961 which was published in the *Herald* (July 24, 1961) titled "Reminiscing on the Auditorium." I am quoting liberally from that article and adding some later published thoughts.

The completion of the Auditorium by next General Conference has the promise of being the most heartwarming experience of my life. This has caused me to look back in retrospect to the many years I have served in the Presiding Bishopric and to the close association I have had with the officers of the church and many others who have contributed to the realization of this goal.

I have been reminded that as early as the 1917 General Conference the need for a General Conference building was emphasized by

President Frederick M. Smith. It was my privilege to have been at that Conference, but as it was somewhat turbulent I—being young and inexperienced—spent just a few days there.

My first real impression of the Auditorium was at the General Conference of 1927. I well remember the Easter morning meeting on the slab (not the floor of the General Conference Chamber) and the General Conference business sessions in the basement below the slab [now the Assembly Room]. It was in one of those sessions that I first began to question the wisdom of the church's undertaking such a venture. The financial condition of the church did not seem to justify a project of such immensity.

At that same Conference I was asked to accept full-time appointment as bishop of Lamoni Stake (I was then serving as bishop of the Minnesota District). I did so but with deep concern as to the financial future of the church and my relationship to it. My family (consisting at that time of my wife and our five-week-old daughter) and I moved to Lamoni on March 1, 1928.

My next outstanding impression of the Auditorium was at the General Conference of 1930, after the superstructure had been erected. This was an outstanding Conference, for it was the centennial anniversary of the organization of the church. A *Herald* report indicated that "there were automobiles from upward to thirty of the states of the union. . . . Boy Scouts counted as many as 1,921 automobiles that were parked."

It was at this Conference that *The Course of Time* composed by John T. Gresty, an evangelist from Australia, was given. The pageant entitled "Fulfillment," with 1,200 in the cast, was another outstanding feature of this Conference. At this Conference President Frederick M. Smith stated, "The Auditorium of Independence is taking its place among the great buildings of our country, and there is a growing pride among Latter Day Saints in this, their greatest building so far erected." He stated further: "It is their building, designed to meet their needs and to promote their welfare."

The Depression Years

The financing and completion of the Auditorium was one of the tasks to which Bishop L. F. P. Curry and I had to give early attention. Because of conditions he did not find it possible to accept full-time appointment until he became counselor to President Smith in 1939. We met together many weekends, giving consideration to the financial policies and their execution. It was a real relief when Bishop N. Ray Carmichael became associated with the Presiding Bishopric in 1934. In those years the Auditorium appeared to some as a "great white elephant." It was about that time that my wife, while coming home from Kansas City on the streetcar one day, heard a couple in the seat back of her commenting about the Auditorium as they passed it. One said to the other, "They'll never finish that building." My wife turned around and said, "Oh, yes they will. It may take time, but they will finish it." To others, who had a vision of its potential (such as Henry C. Smith, the architect, and President Frederick M. Smith who envisioned its eventual service to the church and community), it was essential.

The debt against it was a terrific burden at that time. Bonds had been issued in the total amount of $335,000, but in addition to the mortgage indenture supporting these bonds there was another one which pledged as collateral all properties of the church. Although the debt on the Auditorium was large, it was but a segment of the total debt. I had many interesting experiences in connection with the refinancing of the Auditorium indebtedness, one of which was unique. New bonds were issued on more favorable terms, but we were dependent on the willingness of the bondholders to exchange them for new ones. One day I was called upon by the members of the firm handling this transaction for us to meet with a bondholder who, they said, was determined not to cooperate with us.

When I met with these men, the one holding the bonds looked at me with a calculating eye and said, "I just want to ask you two questions; the first one is, do you realize the seriousness of the financial situation of your church?"

To this I replied, "Yes, I am fully aware of it."

He paused and then said, "Can you tell me whether—if your church is unable to meet its obligations in connection with the Auditorium—I can file a lien against the Stone Church in Independence?"

My answer was, "Sir, I realize that it is within your legal right to file such a lien and, I presume, following it through to its final conclusion you could ultimately collect."

To my surprise, he said, "That is all I want to know, for I have lived in this area most of my life, and I am sure of one thing—you Latter Day Saints will never give up your Stone Church." Then he turned to our financial representatives and said, "I will be glad to make the exchange."

The creditors were for the most part sympathetic and considerate. I always had a deep conviction that the members would respond to the needs of the church and pay off every dollar of debt, and I had no hesitation in so assuring our creditors.

The Auditorium was so designed that, except for some catastrophe such as bombing, it should stand for centuries. Almost from the beginning, however, the architect had peculiar problems. The lot was too small for a building of this size, and he was under the necessity of restricting the size of the area on each end. The Columbian School property was contiguous to the rear of the site, and the front of the building was placed almost on the property line at the front, so the building may not be considered perfect from the standpoint of the offices around the periphery, but no major need was overlooked in the construction of the interior of the oval Conference Chamber with its imposing dome.

In its early days the Auditorium was bleak and unfinished, with tar paper on the front of the building; still I could see beauty in its design. My office then was in the southwest corner of the building on the fifth level. Occasionally, when the pressure got too heavy, I would step into the Conference Chamber at the top of the balcony and visualize its finished beauty as I looked up toward the dome. I found myself impressed with the symmetry of the ribs pointing toward the apex of the ceiling, with the sun throwing its beams on the walls. Lights and shadows enhanced its majesty. In such periods of meditation I gained something of the strength embodied in the building.

Many activities were conducted in the building in its unfinished state. The Harvest Home Festivals held annually in it by volunteers called for the cooperation of hundreds of people and brought to Independence shipments of produce and other products from many places. These proved most helpful in providing for needy people as well as in furthering educational and community progress.

The lower auditorium was used as a recreational facility for youth. An Auditorium orchestra was organized, and many other civic and church activities were carried on, even in those days when the acoustics were not good and the physical appearance of the building was not the most desirable. It also served as a symbol to challenge the Saints to eliminate the debt . . . and as an ensign of Zion.

For many months a picture of the Auditorium with a dark cloud over it (representing the cloud of debt) appeared in the *Herald*. Progress reports were made as funds were received until finally the cloud was eliminated. During this period of time all the councils of the church cooperated, and out of these experiences a unity of purpose and goals developed.

Highlights During the Dark Days

President Frederick M. Smith was always cooperative, although at times he must have become irked with those of us who had the responsibility of financial administration because of our severe application of policy. I was reminded of his many courtesies by a little note found in the *Daily Herald* of April 6, 1932, which called attention to the fact that President Smith was seen carrying lunch trays to Bishop Curry and me because we did not have time to wait in line for our meals.

The Communion services in the Auditorium have always been inspiring. People cooperated to make the building more beautiful through appropriate decorations.

In 1932 a chorus of four hundred and fifty voices, with an orchestra of fifty pieces, gave an outstanding rendition of the *Messiah*.

It is impossible to think of the Auditorium without remembering debt. There were times when people asked me if I thought we would ever get it completed and whether I believed in the ability of the church to pay its debts. I responded with these words upon one occasion: "I am too young a man to jump aboard a sinking ship, and I have no desire to become a martyr to a lost cause." Looking back over the years, I find that I have never had any reason to change my feelings in this respect; and now, while no longer a young man, I look forward with increased hope to this final step of completion of the Auditorium and to even greater steps toward the building of Zion. I pointed this out as far back as 1934, when we were giving consideration to a program for the priesthood, at which time I stated: "We want to build Zion, but every time we begin to work on some practical project, we find our hands tied by debt. We are not our own masters; we are in bondage to debt."

The Saints responded, and we moved steadily toward our goal. Every improvement in the Auditorium was a gratifying achievement: adding the steel railing in the balcony, facing the east and west wings at the front with brick (this was done with bricks from the old Columbian School and finances from the Laurel Club), and completing the foyer, facing the wall supporting the dome with limestone, placing the copper roof on the dome, facing the front walls with limestone, installing the organ, and completing the interior.

Finishing Touches

We had to make a major decision regarding the interior. Should it be dignified and worship-inspiring or utilitarian? We chose the former. Decor and furnishings were important, and we sought advice from experts. Today I never enter the Conference Chamber or the Council Room without a feeling of reverence. I believe God guided us in our decisions.

One day Bishop John Boren, assistant to the Presiding Bishopric in charge of Auditorium construction, asked if I would like to meet the vice-president of the Aeolian Skinner Company who installed the organ. After we were introduced, the man asked, "Bishop, how do you like the organ?" I answered, "I like it, but you are the expert. What do you think of it?" "It is wonderful," he said, "but what is equally important are the acoustics of this building. . . . They are more nearly perfect than in any building I have ever been in."

One wonders how all of this was accomplished. Plans and designs covering every feature of the building had to be discussed and decisions made. Available to us, in addition to Architect Henry C. Smith, was D. Kent Frohwerk of Bloomgarten and Frohwerk, who contributed much in planning and design. We also used other consulting architects and engineers who were specialists in design, acoustics, and materials. All the contractors maintained a high level of workmanship and went beyond the normal requirements of specifications. Franklyn Weddle and his staff, with other consultants, had responsibility in those areas requiring technical and professional knowledge with the organ, music room, and public address system.

Granite for the foyer came from Minnesota and Maine; limestone was shipped from Indiana. Obviously this is a building which, as pointed out by President Frederick M. Smith from the beginning, belongs to all of us.

In 1960 former President Truman spoke to our Men's Club in the Laurel Club Dining Room. Mrs. Truman was with him. After the meeting we invited them to see the General Conference Chamber. He said, "This is one of the finest buildings in this country, and I ought to know, for I have been in most of them."

Step by step we moved toward completion, trying to maintain a high standard of beauty, yet being ever conscious of costs. The ramps and corridors proved a problem of no mean dimension, but completed they too reflect the beauty and dignity commensurate with the rest of the building. The Council Room, administrative and departmental offices, the Assembly Room, the Music Room, the chapel, the dining room, the kitchen, the shop and maintenance department, and the employees' lounge all blend to make a beautiful and functional headquarters building.

There were, of course, questions raised by some which we tried to answer carefully. Two of the most frequently asked were, "Are we not doing too elaborate a job? Isn't the material being used too expensive?" We explained that we could reduce the expense considerably, for example, by just plastering the walls in the foyer, but it would not be such a beautiful or durable entrance. We could have saved money by not providing the glass front and revolving doors. We weighed all these things carefully as we met with the Presidency and the Council of Twelve; the conclusion was that since the

Auditorium was to serve not only present but future generations the savings would not, in the long run, be justified.

Overall Coverage of the Program

The program of debt payment included not only the total debt of the general church and local churches (title to local church property was held in the name of local trustees until the debt was eliminated) and the Auditorium but also the Independence Sanitarium and Hospital and Graceland College. In respect to the Sanitarium, help came from the Independence Chamber of Commerce, which had raised some money prior to 1931. I well remember the charge given me by the late Dr. Charles Allen when I first came to Independence. As we were leaving a meeting of the Chamber he said, "Bishop, I hope the first thing you do is to get the roof on that new building." He was a fine physician and a good supporter of the hospital.

Church members also gave wholehearted support. Thus, through the combined efforts of church and public, the Independence Sanitarium and Hospital was completed.

---

1. Book of Mormon 4:26.
2. F. M. Smith, *Saints' Herald,* February 25, 1931, Editorial.
3. *Saints' Herald,* March 18, 1931, page 243.

Chapter 8

 THE MINISTRY OF THE BISHOPRIC

I was greatly helped throughout the years of my service in the Bishopric in that I had opportunity to review the work of the Presiding Bishops who had preceded me. These were men of integrity, ability, and devotion.

E. L. Kelley served as Presiding Bishop from 1891 to 1916 and established basic principles upon which the work of the church could be conducted. Both he and his successor Benjamin R. McGuire were practicing attorneys-at-law when they accepted church appointment.

Bishop McGuire proved his integrity, capability, and courage in perhaps what may be considered one of the most difficult and trying periods in church history, 1916-1925.

Albert Carmichael, who served from 1925 to 1932, contributed extensively in teaching and developing materials for study in the field of Bishopric functioning.

I have touched upon L. F. P. Curry's fine contribution elsewhere. All the men who preceded me had genuine concern for the church, its ministers, and its members. This was true of my successor, Bishop Walter N. Johnson—1966-1972—and continues with the present Presiding Bishop, Francis E. Hansen.

The ministry of the Bishopric means many things to

different people. In 1926 when I was ordained to the office of bishop, I thought I understood to some extent what the responsibilities might involve. First of all I felt that ordination to the office of bishop had deep spiritual purpose else there would be little significance in those called being ordained to the office of high priest.

As I entered into the work I began to understand the need for an evaluation of the duties which are inherent within the office. While some who were released in the 1930's may have felt that there was little evidence of compassion manifested by the Bishopric, it was nevertheless within our hearts and underlying every administrative act we were required to perform. We felt that the life of the church was at stake, and that those who had sacrificed throughout the years would understand and appreciate the deep concern we had for all who were affected. It was not a pleasant task and, as I have stated elsewhere, had it not been for the spiritual undergirding and faith of the members, the church probably would not have survived.

To convey the deep feeling I had when it became my task to sit down with a man and terminate his service as a full-time appointee to the church is difficult. What could I say to a man who had entered the ministry at twenty-two and served the church in full-time capacity for thirty years? Or a man who, under spiritual impulse and light, had dedicated himself and family to the service of Christ? Those men released from the work they loved were left to make their way in an economic desert. Although the church helped as much as possible, there was no way of mitigating the sorrow that such an experience brought.

Throughout the years these men have remained in my memory, for through them I learned something of the relation of financial administration to the spiritual life of people. And I have said such dire circumstances should never happen again.

But members of the Bishopric do not have full responsibility for that which happens in the church. Nevertheless, they have certain duties and I shall touch upon them as I discuss the areas of bishopric ministry.

President Israel A. Smith called attention to the integration and coordination of the work of the Bishopric with that of other members of the priesthood:

This issue of the *Herald* has been planned to give the church a better idea of the work of the Bishopric at headquarters and throughout the church.

Although this was not our original purpose, it was inevitable that such a presentation would amount to a tribute to those who have served in this important office and to those who are now serving. We join in this tribute. It is well deserved. The members of the Presiding Bishopric and their associates of the Order of Bishops are entitled to the affection and gratitude of the entire church.

The responsibility of voicing the call of those who are to be ordained to the Bishopric rests with the First Presidency. Because of this it is perhaps not inappropriate for us to point out that the work of the Order of Bishops is essentially spiritual. Bishops are first of all high priests. As such, they are shepherds of the souls of men. It is their function to teach us and help us to use our temporal means for spiritual purposes. In the numerous contacts which we have with the Presiding Bishopric in relation to temporal matters, we are happy to find them constantly alert to this basic aspect of their calling. There are many evidences that this is true of the other brethren of the Order.

It may also be well to point out that the work of the Bishopric properly needs to be integrated with that of other members of the priesthood. They are members of a larger team. Motivation for compliance with the financial law grows out of the spiritual life of the people, a product of the total ministry of the church. Although the raising and the administration of finances demands special talents, and properly involves a special calling, all of us must work with the brethren of this Order if their task is to be well and effectively done.

We take great satisfaction in the work of the Bishopric, as we do in that of the other orders and quorums of the priesthood. May God richly bless every man in the office to which he has been called and strengthen us in unity for the sake of his kingdom. I.A.S.—Editorial "The Bishopric Issue," *Saints' Herald*, January 27, 1958, Volume 105, page 74.

In an introductory statement the bishops also emphasized the spiritual nature and motivation of their work:

We of the Bishopric are concerned primarily with the spiritual development of our people. The special responsibilities which are ours in respect to temporalities and the administration of church finance are that they might be sublimated.

We think of the Auditorium not just as a building but as a physical structure which symbolizes the great purpose of the church, which is that of building the kingdom of God. The Gathering, our missionary endeavors, the establishment of the storehouse, our stewardship program, the development of our institutions, the building of houses of worship, all are dependent upon the development of proper attitudes toward wealth. These attitudes are expressed in the payment of the tithe, the giving of offerings, and ultimately the consecration of surplus.

We hope and pray that the fine work of the *Herald* editors in covering the field of the Bishopric may help all of us to understand something of our individual stewardship as members of the church and our collective stewardship as the church corporate.—*Saints' Herald*, January 27, 1958, page 75.

The responsibilities were listed in specific terms:

Financial—Approve and arrange the budgets of appointee families, control of all expenditures in harmony with the Conference-approved budget, care of the poor and needy, investments, approval of houses of worship building programs in conjunction with the First Presidency and apostles concerned and with the local administrative officers, development of the storehouse program, and coordination of institutional financial management with that of the general church.

Real estate—Supervise the land management program,

direction of the church's real estate activity, development of the church's program of building construction, management and care of all church property and historical sites.

Institutions—Coordinate the financial organization of church institutions with that of the General Church: Graceland College, Sanitarium, Central Development Association, Mound Grove Cemetery, Herald House, and Social Service Centers (also general supervision and control of homes for the aged).

Teaching—Develop the teaching and application of the financial law program, implement the stewardship program as it refers to both individuals and groups; also develop personnel for the teaching of the stewardship program through the Aaronic priesthood (such programs are developed with and upon consultation with the First Presidency).

Trustee responsibilities—Serve as trustees in trust for the church. (As such members of the Bishopric are held responsible to the world church or to the subdivision of the church for whose use and benefit the property is held. In this respect they are also subject to the civil laws which provide for such trusteeship. Since the laws in Missouri now allow holding of church property by way of corporations, the Bishopric upon advice from legal counsel and by authority of World Church Conferences may choose to do so.)

General responsibilities—Study and develop the social program of the church in conjunction with community development, counseling, and activating of the gathering program; also encourage the development of individual and family inheritances.

Within the Presiding Bishopric there has always been need for a division of responsibilities. This division is by administrative agreement among the members. Assignments of assistants' work is handled in a similar manner with the approval of the First Presidency and/or when necessary with the approval of the Joint Council.

The Presiding Bishopric also presides over the Order of Bishops. Committees have been appointed from among the order to do research, develop programs for consideration of the Presiding Bishopric and the order, then submit them to other councils concerned—perhaps to the World Conference.

The entire organization of the Bishopric involves many people in many places. The church could not function without the hundreds who serve as bishop's agents and solicitors. The staff members within the office of the Presiding Bishopric who handle the mail and accounts are vitally important too. Actually there is no such thing as a "little man," for every responsibility is important and contributes toward the objective of Zion.

The segregation of funds in harmony with the financial policy of 1932 resulted in the clarification of the nature of assets and liabilities of the church. The Oblation Fund was set up separately. Others, such as the Missionary Reserve Fund, the Houses of Worship Revolving Fund, the Ministerial Reserve Fund, and the Houses of Worship Fund each stood on its own base. There was no intermingling. Previous to 1932 money had been raised for the Graceland College Endowment Fund in the amount of $232,000. This was loaned to the General Church, and an offsetting obligation of that amount was set up in the form of debenture bonds. In 1932 these were recognized as an obligation to Graceland College and included in the debt payment program. The amount raised for the Auditorium was also loaned to the church to meet operating deficits. A mortgage of $335,000 was placed on the Auditorium, with real estate assets hypothecated that proved to be an encumbrance on all the church resources.

The church survived; the financial policy of 1932 worked; and the debt payment in 1943 released the church from bondage. As difficulties were overcome the church again took on spiritual stature, and the missionary force was enlarged. Our people learned about the relation of temporalities to spiritual growth and to the building of Zion. In all of this development the Order of Bishops had a definite part to play, and the order grew in numbers and in ability in financial management. There was also a growing unity within the councils of the church.

Differences, whether between individuals or councils, were readily resolved in the interest of the church as a whole. For the most part this cooperative endeavor continued during the time I served as counselor to Bishop Curry and as Presiding Bishop.

Knowledge of the laws of the church were essential to such unity. I found in the historical record of the life of Joseph Smith III evidence of the task he had to bring orderly procedures into the church and particularly as to the function of the bishops and other councils of the church in relation to one another.

The legal and judicial experience of President I. A. Smith was most helpful in clarifying some questions of law and their interpretations. I have in my personal files some of the correspondence that had to do at one time with the interpretation of Doctrine and Covenants 106 as to the consecration of surplus. President F. M. Smith wrote in approval of an interpretative article by L. F. P. Curry: "It has been apparent to me that attempts to analyze the section wholly within itself, neglecting other passages in our books, are likely to confuse rather than clarify" (*Saints' Herald,* June 29, 1940).

Subsequently, due to the persistent refusal of a few

people to accept the interpretation given, President Israel A. Smith found himself impelled to review the whole matter again. As the law of consecration of surplus was really the issue at stake, and since the church had given its approval in the General Conference action of 1950 to authorize the establishment of the storehouse treasury, President Smith asked me to review with him the whole matter again.

We were not fully in agreement, and President Smith was having difficulty in identifying a certain document to which reference had been made relative to the matter. With the help of F. Henry Edwards, he was finally able to identify it. As a result we wrote a tract titled *The Law of Temporalities.*

It is a matter of importance to the church—particularly as the program for the storehouse is now well under way both by the world church and the stakes. I feel that the article and interpretation will continue to serve as a guide to those who are concerned about the basis of the law when considering surplus. It has been designated on the inside cover of the tract in the following words:

A discussion of the revelations in Doctrine and Covenants on the various aspects of stewardship (Sections 106, 126, 129, etc.) and historical interpretations of the temporal law.

In a growing church changes in personnel take place, converts are added, and with the growth in membership there is sometimes a tendency to lose sight of some of the experience of the church in previous years. Often issues are discussed which seem to be totally new. However, in reviewing the history of the church one can see that issues usually revolve around the interpretation of the laws and policies of the church and the difference in the personalities of those interpretations of the past with those of the present. Laws, in most respects, are based on the total experience of forebears in relation to contemporary conditions and needs.

I shall touch briefly upon a function of the Bishopric in respect to trusteeship of the properties of the church. Joseph Smith, Jr., and Joseph Smith III were greatly concerned about safeguarding the church in respect to the functions of quorums so as to have certain checks and balances that would protect the rights of all people.

Of necessity, there are presidents, or presiding offices, growing out of, or appointed of, or from among those who are ordained to the several offices in these two priesthoods.

Of the Melchisedec priesthood, three presiding high priests, chosen by the body, appointed and ordained to that office, and upheld by the confidence, faith, and prayer of the church, form a quorum of the Presidency of the church.

The twelve traveling councilors are called to be the Twelve Apostles, or special witnesses of the name of Christ, in all the world; thus differing from other officers in the church in the duties of their calling.

And they form a quorum equal in authority and power to the three presidents previously mentioned.

The seventy are also called to preach the gospel, and to be especial witnesses unto the Gentiles and in all the world—thus differing from other officers in the church in the duties of their calling; and they form a quorum equal in authority to that of the twelve especial witnesses, or apostles, just named.

And every decision made by either of these quorums must be by the unanimous voice of the same; that is, every member in each quorum must be agreed to its decisions, in order to make their decisions of the same power or validity one with the other.—Doctrine and Covenants 104:11a-f.

Reference to the preceding was made by Joseph Smith III in the following:

An ecclesiasticism in which there is a centralization of power in a ruling head may be as dangerous to the liberties of the people in a spiritual sense as a kingly rule of despotism may be to political and temporal welfare. Priestcraft is subversive of the good of those over whom it rules. The idea that the priesthood can do no wrong, or that all the words and acts of a spiritual ruler are directed by divine wisdom and power, is a dangerous fallacy, and wherever either becomes a rule of acceptance of what is said or done and forms a basis of action on the part of the people bad results are sure to follow. Just as a king may become corrupt and turn his rule into unequal and evil ways for self-aggrandizement and oppression, so may evil creep in and take captive the priestly ruler and make merchandise of the people's rights and subvert their liberties to selfish ends.

History confirms these propositions.

In the restoration of the gospel by the discovery of the Book of Mormon and the revival of the principle of revelation, the Lord has been mindful of the result to his people of the rule of kings and priests in wickedness. Whatever may have been the rules of organization and procedure in church government as set forth in the Bible and in religious bodies, abundant safeguards have been provided to secure the people against encroachment on the part of irresponsible rulers. There is no need to discuss the "divine right of kings to rule." The Lord has said "in time ye shall have no king on this land." This takes this danger out of the way. Is there danger from priestcraft? Joseph Smith, the Seer, wrote, "If any man exercises his priesthood in any degree of unrighteousness," "amen to that man's priesthood." This shows that God does not intend that what he conferred to bless men should be used to subvert their faith or destroy their liberties.

One of the earliest revelations given at the very beginning recognized the necessity for distinctive organizations within the body; holding one common priesthood—right to act—and having different offices acting in harmony each with every other for the establishment and carrying out of one common object.

The setting for this revelation is given in the preface to Section 104.

For the sake of brevity I shall not quote the whole article written by Joseph Smith III, but enough—together with some other references—to indicate the extent to which he was concerned about the future of the church.

In order that the people may be safe from the undue advantage of the position accorded to this leading quorum in case ambition seize them or any one of them to the overriding of the integrity of the others, two other quorums composed of larger numbers are provided, the members of which quorums hold the same priesthood as these presiding officers, each quorum being invested with equal authority in decision, so that if the three presidents should attempt to take from the people any, or all, the liberties that membership in the church entitles them to, it is in the power of the Twelve and Seventy to check such ambition and secure the people from imposition.

Should either quorum attempt to introduce into the corporate body false doctrine, or to institute what would vitiate the spiritual life of the people, whether such effort arose from the spontaneous action of the quorum, or was the result of the ambitious efforts of one to serve the ends of selfish desire to rule, such attempt may be met by the other two and must fail of effect.

There are three in the first quorum, twelve in the second, there may be thirty-six, or four hundred and ninety members in the third. In the church as now organized there are about one hundred and thirty in the Seventy, one full quorum and one nearly full. No measure tending to the subversion of the liberties of the people, originating in either quorum, could possibly pass the scrutiny of the other two, unless there should be such collusion between the membership of all of them as is inconceivable under the light of present information and personal integrity known to exist in these several quorums. We know of no body of religionists having an organized existence the membership of which is so amply safeguarded against extreme imposition from misguided or ambitious men as is the Church of Jesus Christ organized April 6, 1830, by virtue of divinely enacted organic laws given to govern its spiritual existence and continuation. Joseph Smith, President Reorganized Church.—*Saints' Herald,* Volume 52, March 22, 1905.

I have felt on at least two occasions that the timely calling for a convening of the three quorums of concurrent juristiction might have averted some of the catastrophic divisiveness within the church and could well be a procedure that might assure cohesiveness for the future. One of the freedoms that we enjoy in the Restoration church is that of thinking about and discussing matters such as this.

In another article in the *Herald* for September 6, 1954, President Israel A. Smith made this introductory statement to "A Letter of Instruction" issued by his father in the *Herald* of March 13, 1912.

Inasmuch as this "letter" has been accorded general recognition as a correct statement of law as to the selection of a successor "in the case of the death of a president of the church, or his removal for cause, and has guided the procedure and action of General Church officers and the General Conference, and as we have frequent inquiries respecting the matter, we have deemed it wise to reproduce this "letter of instruction" in its entirety, notwithstanding the space required. . . .

I remember clearly that the author of this "letter," in his last illness, expressed his satisfaction that he had anticipated the need of the church for such instruction. Israel A. Smith.

In that letter there is reaffirmation of the rightness of provision for such quorum functioning:

From what is given from the authority cited above, it is clear that in authorizing the organization of the church, the Lord provided an ample safeguard against imposition upon the people from the improper aspiration of any of the leading authorities of the church, by establishing three quorums as checks and counter checks upon each other, the three being equal in authority in matters of importance, neither one of the three being paramount to overriding the authority of the other two. . . .

The following is another illustration from Part II of this letter (*Herald* of September 13, 1954, page 887):

The church is not at liberty to accept or to follow the precedent supposedly established by the action of the quorum of twelve in the fall of 1844, in the Twelve taking absolute charge of the administration of the affairs of the church which culminated in 1847 in the installing of a Presidency by taking three from the then nine adhering members of the Twelve existing at the death of the Prophet and installing them in the Presidency of the church with Brigham Young as their chief, which action was followed by public proclamation of the plural marriage dogma with its concomitant corruptions of the doctrines of the church, through the revelation and the restoration of the gospel.

This reaffirmation with other supporting evidences which

have come by way of revelation and General Conference enactments support the basic laws of the church regarding rights and responsibilities of various quorums.

At a critical time in the history of the church when the question of responsibility of the Presiding Bishop as trustee arose Israel A. Smith discussed the matter in an article titled "Know the Law" (*Herald* for November 26, 1924). Although he wrote this when he was counselor to Presiding Bishop Benjamin R. McGuire, he maintained the same position when he became a member of the First Presidency and also president of the church. He not only discussed the matter in relation to civil law but also quoted from an article of Joseph Smith III published in the *Herald* of May 29, 1901:

> The Book of Covenants provides that the church should hold its properties through its Bishopric, and not through the Presidency as trustee. This makes the Bishop the trustee of church properties. To hold property in other ways is not in accord with church rule. . . . The law provides for ways of dealing with the Bishopric, but does not so provide for trustees other than the Bishopric.
>
> There was a greater element of danger to the General Church in the way of putting its properties into the control of the President, than in the Bishopric rule. The control of the finances of the church added to the spiritual control would be an element of mischief to the general body, if the President was an ambitious and unscrupulous man, as the rules applying to the care of the finances under the Bishopric would not apply to him, and he would be in a way an irresponsible agent.

President W. Wallace Smith in a letter dated January 4, 1972, and addressed to all appointees made the following statement in regard to trusteeship:

> As trustees in trust for the church, the Presiding Bishopric hold title to church properties and are held responsible to the World Church or to the subdivision of the church for whose use and benefit the property is held. As trustees in trust they are legally responsible to the World Conference for all the financial assets of the World Church. It is recognized that they will use discretionary judgment in the manage-

ment of the temporal resources of the church as they fulfill the requirements of the fiduciary relationship.

In times when many ideas spring from many people, it seems wise to cover this phase of the Bishopric responsibility as a stimulation to further research by those who may be called upon at some time to consider the relationships of quorums to quorums as they pertain to the business of the church in stake and General Conferences.

Revelations such as Section 126 (particularly paragraph 10) have bearing on such matters.

In my own experience in the Bishopric I found there were times when we felt it advisable to seek the advice of the Standing High Council in addition to that of the Joint Council. It was always the policy of the Bishopric, of course, to work in close association with the First Presidency.

In Appreciation

Throughout the years I served in the Presiding Bishopric I deeply appreciated the loyal, devoted, and highly capable help of members of the Bishopric staff.

Without such support the task would have been too great. I wish I could list all who have contributed, but this is not possible. In mentioning a few I am not unaware or unappreciative of the others who served. These few represent a particular contribution that has extended over a long period of time.

N. Ray Carmichael—with whom I worked closely both in Lamoni, Iowa, and as co-counselor to Presiding Bishop L. F. P. Curry—eventually took over the responsibility as manager of church farms. He also gave excellent counsel for many years regarding land purchase and operational management.

Carrol L. Olson—lawyer, accountant, and counselor—gave

unreservedly of his time and ability from 1931 up to the date of his death in 1972.

Rosamond Sherman served most efficiently and graciously as my secretary for over a period of thirty years.

Others who gave exceptional service over an equally long period of time were Roberta McPherson, Odess Athey, and August Witte. Two others who served in the office of the Presidency and were dear to the hearts of members of the Bishopric were Oscar W. Newton and Gladys Gould.

Chapter 9

 IMPLEMENTING OUR SOCIAL IDEALS

As one tries to interpret the teachings of Christ he is immediately brought to the realization that the social aspects of the gospel are so inherent in his teachings as to make their application essential to the well-rounded development of personality, and that service is basic to the attainment of the abundant life of which Jesus spoke.

When we think of social ideals, we too frequently do so in generalities. Jesus spoke time and again of those things which were specific. He taught the need of clothing the naked, of feeding the hungry, of visiting the sick. He stressed the development of faith, righteous judgment, love, forgiveness, repentance, and humility. He emphasized the importance of sowing good seed on good ground. By example he showed the need of ministering to the backslider or the lost sheep and inculcated in his disciples the importance of wise stewardship.

In all of this there was revealed that a man's life consists not of the abundance of things which he possesses but the use he makes of them and his attitude toward that use. It should not seem strange that in the revelations which came to this church there should be both reiteration and reemphasis on these basic principles and fundamentals to guide those called to the specific task of building Christ's kingdom on the earth.

To Latter Day Saints, the call to follow Christ means more than consideration of his teachings in ritualistic and liturgical form. There must be some expression of belief in him through the avenue of service, and there is scarcely an area in human need that does not require the attention of the church.

In the year 1967 a study by government was made of poverty as it existed among both blacks and whites. The solution to their problem depends on the development not only of those who are qualified in the fields of government and economics but those who are impelled by a sense of responsibility for the welfare of their fellowmen.

Despite all of the agencies of social welfare, the need for the church to continue to work toward the attainment of its objectives becomes increasingly more obvious when the list of needs is measured against accomplishments. I have learned, through my many years of public service, that it takes "a mile of effort to make an inch of social progress."

The problems are not easily solved by legislation. They call for the application of gospel principles which Jesus taught—tolerance, charity, sympathy, patience, and the will to exemplify Christian love and brotherhood. These crises can best be met by the action of individuals committing themselves to specific objectives which are basic to the cause of the kingdom. That is the reason for the church—to call men to service, and through service to eternal life.

Our challenge today is to carry the gospel of goodwill to all nations of the earth. Although some have felt that we were on the verge of disaster, I personally think we shall not only survive but move forward continuously toward the building of the kingdom. I may be considered an idealist or a dreamer when I say that our salvation lies in our commitment to a great cause and in subordinating our lives to goals which are designed to bring equality of opportunity and a better life to all.

While vast wealth remains in the hands of a relative few, much is controlled by those of lesser means. It is to both that the call to become good stewards for Jesus Christ is issued. It is to such that the storehouse with its provision for inheritance and help for the needy will have meaning.

THE GATHERING

The current objective of this movement is the gathering of church members into various nuclei, with Independence, Missouri, as the center place. This gathering is a continuous process. It is the mobilization in central areas of those with special qualifications, making possible the development of highly specialized staffs. In addition to serving in the Center Place, these may be assigned to specific areas to further the interests of the church or to stabilize groups, branches, and districts. The outreach must always be motivated by evangelism if the church is to become a stable, vital, dynamic body.

There are many groups with different goals, among which are the minorities that seek to establish themselves on a higher plateau than they have experienced in the past. This includes those of the black race, who for centuries have not had their proper place because of prejudice and lack of equal opportunity, and the Jews who, after centuries of being a "scattered nation," have now established the Zionist movement. And there are the Indians who as a race once populated America; they are now fighting alleged wrongs of the past as well as those of the present. Women, while not a minority, are seeking greater freedom, more opportunities for recognition, and positions once relegated only to men. Other groups, smaller in numbers, also are protesting their being overlooked or neglected.

The Latter Day Saint movement also represents a minority group. It has a record of loyalty to government, of persecution in its early days, of overcoming prejudice, continued adherence to objectives which were established at its inception. One of the most important of these objectives is the gathering of those who accepted the theology and philosophy of the church founded by Joseph Smith, Jr.

Belief in the gathering as a divine process is evidenced in the early revelations which were accepted as authentic by the church as a body.

Listen to the voice of Jesus Christ, your Redeemer, the great I AM, whose arm of mercy hath atoned for your sins, who will gather his people even as a hen gathereth her chickens under her wings.—Doctrine and Covenants 28:1 (see also 98:5).

Spiritual enlightenment characterized the Restoration movement in respect to new concepts of God, of his present concern for humanity, and of the need for the gathering of God's people.

The prophetic words of Jesus recorded in Matthew 24:14 have significant meaning for those in this present generation who believe in the ultimate accomplishment of the divine will among men: "And this gospel of the kingdom shall be preached in all the world, for a witness unto all nations, and then shall the end come" (24:32, Inspired Version).

From the beginning of the Restoration movement attempts have been made by the people of the church to gather in certain areas to fulfill the law more completely. The first movement of any consequence was at Kirtland, Ohio. This settlement, however, was not designated as one of permanency in the sense that Kirtland was Zion, although some thought that it was to be at least a cornerstone: "I say unto you that you are now called immediately to make a solemn proclamation of my gospel, and of this stake which I have planted to be a corner stone of Zion, which shall be polished with that refinement which is after the similitude of a palace" (Doctrine and Covenants 107:1b).

S. A. Burgess, in a *Herald* article titled "The Gathering—The Location of Zion," ascribes the location of Zion as centering in Independence, Missouri.

The positive evidence goes to the pointing out of a certain location for Zion, her stakes and the regions round about. . . . In 1830 certain of the brethren proceeded to the land of Missouri. In January, 1831, they apparently located in Western Missouri, in Kaw Township, Zion.—Volume 64, page 889.

One of the most important revelations on the subject of Zion prophesies its fulfillment:

Righteousness and truth will I cause to sweep the earth as with a flood, to gather out my own elect from the four quarters of the earth unto a place which I shall prepare; a holy city, that my people may gird up their loins, and be looking forth for the time of my coming; for there shall be my tabernacle, and it shall be called Zion, a New Jerusalem.—Doctrine and Covenants 36:12f, g.

In the 1970 edition of the Doctrine and Covenants this explanatory statement precedes the revelation:

In June 1830 Joseph Smith began an inspired correction of the Holy Scriptures, the necessity for which had been pointed out in the revelation of June 1830 (D. and C. 22:24). While engaged in this work in December 1830, Joseph received the following revelation which is an extract from the prophecy of Enoch. This revela-

tion now forms Genesis 7:1-78 of the Inspired Version of the Holy
Scriptures. . . .

The promise which came to the church at that time
has been cherished by its members. It specifically calls
them to righteousness. In it the kingdom is defined in
these words: "The Lord called his people Zion, because
they were of one heart and one mind, and dwelt in
righteousness. . . ."

Various occurrences are foretold: "Great tribulation
shall be among the children of men. . . . Righteousness will
I send down out of heaven. . . . Truth will I send forth
out of the earth. . . ." These promises hold out hope for
those who have caught the vision of the possibility of a
righteous community and give meaning to the revelations
calling for the gathering:

And now concerning the gathering, let the bishop and the
agent make preparations for those families which have been commanded to come to this land, as soon as possible, and plant them
in their inheritance.—Doctrine and Covenants 57:6a.

More particularly the designation of the beginning of
the gathering is specified: "Behold, the place which is
now called Independence, is the Center Place, and the
spot for the temple is lying westward upon a lot which is
not far from the courthouse" (57:1d).

The revelation which followed the call to gather contained this directive:

Firstly, the rich and the learned, the wise and the noble; and
after that cometh the day of my power; then shall the poor, the
lame, and the blind, and the deaf, come in unto the marriage of
the Lamb, and partake of the supper of the Lord, prepared for the
great day to come. Behold, I, the Lord, have spoken it.—58:3e, f.

The gathering held out certain benefits to members of
the church, but such promises were also conditional:

Now this commandment I give unto my servants, for their benefit while they remain, for a manifestation of my blessings upon their heads, and for a reward of their diligence, and for their security for food and for raiment, for an inheritance; for houses and for lands, in whatsoever circumstances I, the Lord, shall place them; and whithersoever I, the Lord, shall send them.–70:4a, b (1831).

Undoubtedly the Saints were anxiously inquiring about the land which had been designated as Zion in July 1831. An interesting description of it is given in Volume I, Church History, pages 207-209 (*Times and Seasons,* Volume 5, page 450):

Unlike the timbered states in the East, except upon the rivers and water courses, which were verdantly dotted with trees from one to three miles wide, as far as the eye can glance, the beautiful rolling prairies lay spread around like a sea of meadows. The timber is a mixture of oak, hickory, black walnut, elm, cherry, honey locust, mulberry, coffee bean, hackberry, box elder, and basswood, together with the addition of cottonwood, buttonwood, pecan, soft and hard maple, upon the bottoms. . . . The soil is rich and fertile, from three to ten feet deep, and generally composed of rich black mold, intermingled with clay and sand. . . .

This is accompanied by a detailed description regarding livestock, wild game, bees, and other natural resources. The location is given in longitude, latitude, and distance in relation to the Allegheny and Rocky Mountains. Its future is described as "most blessed"; further, "were the virtues of the inhabitants only equal to the blessings of the Lord, which he permits to crown the industry and efforts of those inhabitants, there would be a measure of the good things of life, for the benefit of the saints, full, pressed down and running over, even an hundredfold." There is mention of shortcomings, but the promise is held out "concerning Zion in the last days how the glory of Lebanon is to come upon her."

I have previously related how as a boy I listened to the missionaries who came to visit us from time to time. They told us of the sacrifices and devotion of the first ministers of the church as they moved westward. All were motivated by what they envisioned—the development of a brotherhood wherein Christians could associate together in a common cause. Some of these men were inclined to be a little overzealous. They tried to persuade my parents that the "hastening time" was upon us and that we should flee to Zion. My father took the position that church law called for the gathering to be on a systematic basis—which was in keeping with the way God worked. He pointed out that the establishment of Zion would require decades of preparation and a depth of experience; therefore haste was ill-advised.

In the 1830's the men who moved from New York to Kirtland and from Kirtland to Independence endured many hardships. When I think of what I might have done had I faced a situation similar to theirs I can only conclude that one having deep convictions relative to the will and purpose of God can undertake almost any project or goal if he has the assurance that he is moving in harmony with the divine will. The dangers and difficulties they encountered were endurable because of their sincere belief in the church.

The movement of the gathering definitely centered around Independence. Here the church sought to establish itself on a permanent basis. S. A. Burgess in a *Saints' Herald* article (Volume 64) referred to a series of pamphlets written by Orson Pratt after the death of Joseph the Martyr, from which he quoted:

But where is the spot where the city of Zion or the New Jerusalem shall stand? We answer, in Jackson County, Missouri, on the western

194

frontier of the United States. It is there that the city of Zion shall be built. All the other cities that have been built by the gathering of the Saints are called, not Zion, but stakes of Zion.

Two excerpts from *The Story of the Church* describe the territory and the people around Independence. Charles Joseph Latrobe, an Englishman traveling in North America, described Independence in these words:

The Town of Independence was full of promise like most of the innumerable towns springing up in the midst of the forests of the West, many of which, though dignified by high-sounding epithets, consist of nothing but a ragged congeries of five or six rough log huts, two or three clapboard houses, two or three so-called hotels, alias grog-shops, a few stores, a bank, a printing office, and a barnlike church. It [Independence] lacked at the time I commemorate, the last three edifices, but was nevertheless a thriving and aspiring place, in its way. . . .

Washington Irving wrote his sister, Mrs. Paris, from the hotel:

The fertility of all this western country is truly remarkable. The soil is like that of a garden, and the luxuriance and beauty of the forests exceed any I have ever seen. We have gradually been advancing, however, to rougher and rougher life, and we are now at a straggling little frontier village that has only been five years in existence. . . .

As he viewed this country Joseph Smith saw the tremendous opportunities it presented, but he was also concerned about the people and sensed keenly the social responsibility of the Saints:

Our reflections were great, coming as we did from a highly cultivated society in the East, and standing now upon the confines or western limits of the United States and looking into the vast wilderness of those who wait in darkness. How natural it was to note the degradation, leanness of intellect, ferocity and jealousy of a people that were nearly a century behind the time, and to feel for those who roamed about without the benefit of civilization, refinement, or religion.—*Story of the Church,* page 118.

195

The Saints immediately started schools, the first in Jackson County. Oliver Cowdery and Parley P. Pratt were both teachers, the first schoolteachers in Jackson County. Ziba Peterson is reported to have opened a school at Lone Jack.—*Ibid.,* page 134.

One wonders why it was that these people, moving westward with high ideals, hopes, and aspirations, with definite desire to improve the country, met so much opposition and often even persecution. Perhaps the factor which caused the most prejudice was the Saints' attitude toward slavery.

There is evidence to intimate that after extensive missionary campaigning in the South, a few slaveholders with their slaves moved into Nauvoo, perhaps even in Caldwell County, Missouri. Slavery existed in a limited degree in the Utah Mormon church previous to the Civil War. But it may safely be said that the predominant sentiment was against it. Doniphan cites it as the chief cause of the Jackson County troubles.—*Ibid.,* page 137.

One of the next important steps taken by church members was the establishing of a printing plant in Independence. This was largely for the publication of a paper, *The Evening and Morning Star,* and for publishing the revelations given to the church, *The Book of Covenants.*

Another important development also was taking place. Edward Partridge, who had been called to be bishop of the church in February 1831, was directing the purchasing of land. Instructions had been given to the church to purchase land, and on December 10, 1831, "for the consideration of one hundred and thirty dollars," he bought a tract including the spot which Joseph Smith had pointed out in August 1831 as the location for the temple. He also secured approximately two thousand acres, some by purchase and some by original entry.

Title records reveal that herein lay some of the elements of conflict, for side by side on the records covering contiguous tracts of ground were the names of Edward Partridge and Lilburn W. Boggs who later issued the extermination order for the Saints.

Partridge's rather enormous purchases of land were not for himself, but to be allotted as inheritances to the Saints who came up to Zion to aid in the establishment of the new economic system, variously known as the "United Order," the "Zionic Plan," and the "Order of Enoch."—*Story of the Church,* page 153.

Such economic planning with religious motivation was not peculiar to Latter Day Saints. Other groups attempted to apply stewardship principles to land ownership and community life. Much research is necessary to obtain a comprehensive picture of the growth and prosperity of Latter Day Saints in the land of Zion and of the opposition which developed. Neither mob violence nor persecution deterred the Saints from following their convictions, promulgating the gospel of Jesus Christ, and seeking to build the kingdom in harmony with their understanding of the divine purpose.

The church grew; missionaries increased in numbers; missionary work was continually broadened; and leaders were added to the church who figure prominently in its history. The church doctrine which was developed was quite comprehensive as to life to be experienced here and life which was to continue hereafter. Faith, repentance, baptism, laying on of hands, belief in the resurrection, and eternal judgment were the fundamentals of the gospel of this new church. All of these were to be expressed and broadened in these concepts of Zion and stewardship.

Despite opposition and persecution the Saints persisted in furthering their program of the gathering. It seems to me that their only counterparts are the Jewish people.

The Restoration movement, which has as its core a gathered people living "in the world but not of it," is premised on the need for world brotherhood. It is both a philosophy and an ideal, calling men to build new communities and restore old ones.

On June 25, 1833, Joseph Smith sent from Kirtland the plat of the new City of Zion, but it was never used. Historical records indicate that careful planning had been given to the laying out of the City of Zion. Provision was made for public buildings and houses; the streets were to be over one hundred feet wide, and all the buildings were to be of brick or stone. These plans, together with the ones developed for Kirtland and Nauvoo, bear record of the vision and ability of those who were seeking to build new communities, but their hopes were to be realized only in part. The Saints were driven out of Independence; the printing office was destroyed. The disaster is described by Inez Smith Davis in *The Story of the Church:*

It was now the summer of 1833. Immigration had poured into the County of Jackson in great numbers; and the church in that county numbered upward of one thousand souls. These had all purchased lands and paid for them, and most of them were improving in buildings and cultivation. . . .

Perhaps more than all else contributing to the mob of July 20, 1833, in Independence, was the publication of an editorial "Free People of Color," in *The Evening and Morning Star* of that month. . . .

Upon the 20th a petition was drawn up and signed, asking . . . that the Latter Day Saints leave Jackson County. . . . The brick printing office was torn down [it was located on what is now the corner of Liberty and Lexington]. . . . Type and papers were scattered along the streets. . . . The press and most of the type were carried to the river and thrown in. [Bishop Partridge was tarred and feathered.]

On July 23, 1833, a treaty was signed. . . . The Latter Day Saints agreed to leave the county.—Pages 167, 174-177.

Hardships continued to follow the Saints as they fled to Clay and Caldwell counties. A military regiment was formed under the laws of the state with Lyman Wight as the commanding officer. Other Mormon settlements spread into Daviess, Livingston, Clinton, and Carroll counties.

At Far West the new community was planned with W. W. Phelps and John Whitmer holding title to the land one mile square. Persecution, mob murder at Haun's Mill, the arrest of Joseph Smith, Lyman Wight, and others, and the continued harassments finally drove the Saints to Nauvoo.

From revelations in the Doctrine and Covenants it is apparent that Independence is the central area from which all Zionic endeavors stem. Since the ideal community originally planned did not materialize some may feel that the opportunity has passed, for since these revelations were given many changes have taken place. The Lord recognizes changing conditions and makes provision from time to time for such additional light as may be necessary to enable the church to adjust to them. A revelation received through Joseph Smith III in 1909 clarifies and supplements preceding revelations pertaining to the gathering:

The conditions surrounding the work, the increase of the membership of the church, the increasing desire for gathering together, and the necessity existing for the obtaining places for settlement in the regions round about, under the existing laws of the United States, and especially the state of Missouri, require that the Bishopric be authorized to take such measures as will bring to pass the organization of those who are desirous and willing to form parts in colonization under terms of association in different localities where settlements may be made and may lawfully secure and hold property for the benefit of themselves and their fellow church members and the whole body of the church when organized.—Doctrine and Covenants 128:1a-c.

In the eighth paragraph provision is made for the work to be carried on by the Saints within the framework of present society:

The Spirit saith further: That these organizations contemplated in the law may be effected and the benefits to be derived therefrom be enjoyed by the Saints, in such enjoyment they can not withdraw themselves so completely from a qualified dependence upon their Gentile neighbors surrounding them as to be entirely free from intercommunication with them; yet it is incumbent upon the Saints while reaping the benefits of these organizations to so conduct themselves in the carrying into operation the details of their organizations as to be *in the world but not of it.* —128:8a, b.

With this as the basis for consideration of the work to be carried on in the central area to fulfill the purpose of the Restoration, we might view the minimum as providing a nucleus around which a Zionic community can be developed which will give a fuller expression of Christian brotherhood (Church Objectives adopted by the General Conference of 1932).

Today, however, we are faced with the problem of implementing the principles of social and economic organization that served as the basis for the endeavors of those who came to Independence in the 1830's. To think that the same approach could be made that was made by the early Saints would be as fallacious as to think that any segment of our society could be transplanted back to the locale and environment of those pioneer days. This we cannot do, but if we could, I am sure that very few would care to participate in such a venture.

INHERITANCE

An inheritance is that which a man requires to exercise responsible stewardship of self and family. This will vary according to his home, or its equivalent, depending on his circumstances in life, his needs, his capacity to manage, and his ability to acquire. Through the application of the principles of needs and just wants, inheritances are kept within the bounds of equity and justice.

Education may also be considered as a part of one's inheritance, for normally it provides the resources such as knowledge, skills, and disciplines which are essential to competency in providing for necessities.

When we were emerging from the depression the problems pertaining to individuals acquiring inheritances were of necessity brought into the foreground of our thinking. Many people lost their homes through mortgage foreclosures, and others consumed their savings in providing the basic necessities of life. Under these conditions, the possibility of everyone acquiring an inheritance seemed remote.

War sometimes speeds up the tempo of progress. Out of World War II came the revitalizing of our economy which brought employment and increased income to thousands of people. However, the individuals acquiring inheritances did not keep up with the increase in population; housing and capital for many were still in short supply. Today, despite the obvious accumulation of wealth, there continues to be the wide gap between the well-to-do and the underprivileged.

In the approach being made here to the subject of inheritance, we should give some consideration to the principle as it is outlined in the scriptures. There is ample evidence in sacred literature that the right of inheritance in respect to wealth, as well as spiritual qualities, depends on compliance with the fundamentals of the gospel law. This is particularly true of those promises which refer to the right of citizenship in the kingdom of God.

Frequently we talk about the wonderful benefits which are to accrue from building the kingdom while disregarding the fact that these can be realized only when individuals develop the capacity to acquire both physical and spiritual resources. These may be passed down from one generation to the next. They also may be used to meet the current needs of society.

Every individual has the right—in fact the responsibility—to acquire an inheritance. In both the Old and New Testaments the transferring of spiritual and physical inheritances is acknowledged as a normal experience of life. (While spiritual inheritances may be acquired and passed on from generation to generation, our primary consideration here has to do with property. It is apparent, however, that there are spiritual values realized through the proper utilization and distribution of physical resources.)

Inheritance is related to the subject of equality. The sharing of physical resources through proper distribution always has attached to it the problem of equity. The core of the Restoration movement is the promulgation of a philosophy that puts into proper relationship the physical and the spiritual. This principle was enunciated by Jesus when he was approached by the young man who asked, "What good thing shall I do, that I may have eternal life?" Jesus replied, "If thou wilt be perfect, go, sell that thou hast, and give to the poor, and thou shalt have treasure in heaven, and come and follow me" (Matthew 19:16, 21). No one is perfect, but the road is visible and the direction is clear.

Church law is specific; it states that individuals and families should have inheritances according to their needs. Albert Carmichael, on pages 40 and 41 of his *Elements of Stewardship and Our Social Program,* stated:

The inheritance consists of property in our possession and for which we hold a title or deed.

Inheritances are divided into two classes:

A. Real Estate

B. Personal Property

The investment of the title to this real estate and personal property depends upon

A. Its service

B. The needs

Bishop Carmichael further emphasized the relationship between inheritances and stewardships, placing inheritance in secondary importance. He pointed out that stewardship might include the management of property constituting the inheritance as well as other properties over which the steward had control or management responsibility. He maintained that one usually should hold title to that which is his inheritance.

I, the Lord, stretched out the heavens, and builded the earth as a very handy work; and all things therein are mine; and it is my purpose to provide for my saints, for all things are mine; but it must needs be done in mine own way; and, behold, this is the way, that I, the Lord, have decreed to provide for my saints: that the poor shall be exalted, in that the rich are made low; for the earth is full, and there is enough and to spare.—Doctrine and Covenants 101:2d-f.

The scriptures certainly emphasize that in God's creation there is enough for everyone, and if there is conformance with his law all needs can be met. One cannot help asking, "Will man destroy God's creation through waste, spoilage, and disregard for the rights of others, or will the principles of the gospel ultimately prevail?"

Laws have been enacted by governments to place arbitrary limitations on individuals and groups to prevent economic control on the part of a few over their fellowmen, but today great monopolies and conglomerates ignore or circumvent the basic purpose of these laws. Part of this is due to the fact that too few individuals are willing to assume responsibilities of executive and administrative nature, preferring instead to follow the easy course.

While certain standards may be developed out of the common experience we gain as we move forward in our economic organization, it would appear that these arbitrary limitations may not be placed unless there is equal consideration given to individual needs and requirements on the basis of responsibilities assumed. Normal standards may be developed only out of our experience and through our willingness to exert a self-discipline which will keep us within certain boundaries which are determined by the common weal of others.

The factors having a bearing on these standards are geographical location and area. The metropolitan and industrial centers require a minimum standard of living different from that in agricultural areas. This is also true respecting the middle-size cities and communities which are neither industrial nor rural. Thus to say, for instance, that an inheritance of a certain fixed value or sum should be applied to all is to ignore the basic factors underlying our total problem.

The solution can come only through complete compliance on the part of individuals with the temporal law of the church, which requires first of all the accounting from which may be determined the essentials for the welfare, growth, and ultimate security (in the economic sense) of each individual.

Inheritance and the Storehouse

Inheritances may be small or large in proportion to the extent that the economic affairs of the individual may be related to the activities and the work of the storehouse. The point of beginning, both as to inheritance and organization of the storehouse, is that of the accounting. The importance of this is not as well understood as will be necessary if real progress is to be made in the organization of economic life, for it is through the process of accounting that the immediate status of the individual is determined and his individual course charted.

It seems a relatively simple process, yet it is only partially understood by many and not complied with by others. The filing of the tithing statement is the first step in stewardship accounting. The next step in accounting is the allocation of funds beyond the obligation of tithing. Such an allocation may consist of specific offerings the steward wishes to make other than those which may be determined as surplus. Allocation of surplus may be made after one's inheritance is provided.

The steward should apply for and fill out the "Surplus and Analysis and Agreement Form" (No. PB-5-71). From the information thus obtained he may plan goals and designate that which should constitute an inheritance.

The amount and composition of the inheritance and the computation of surplus for the storehouse can be determined through the planning of the individual and the Bishopric.

It is my belief that when group stewardship associations are formed, these should function in allocating surplus to and through stake storehouses rather than through interrelations among themselves. The present interpretation of the Bishopric is that storehouse organization is limited to "those approved as stake or world church program objectives" (Form PB-5-71, page 4). This is a sound policy, for throughout the years small groups have attempted such programs without adequate resources or personnel. With the growth of the church stakes are increasing in number, and through stake organization personnel for the initiation and supervision of programs have become available. Economic relations within or among groups also may be coordinated through stake storehouse organization.

It seems logical that stake storehouses should function on the basis of "freedom from debt" as moneys consecrated to the storehouse are "trust funds" that will require administering in harmony with the purpose for which they are consecrated.

Freedom from debt should be complete with the exception of current liabilities which may exist in the operation of the storehouse business. Even for these there should be assets available. This position may be considered extreme, but the whole principle of the storehouse is that of consecration of economic surplus for productive purposes.

To illustrate more fully, individual or corporate businesses use the terminology of surplus in the accounting sense, which applies to that portion of capital accumulated above the capital stock liability and all other liabilities existing. Surplus in the economic sense is that which has been produced over and above both needs and liabilities.

The revelations to the church were quite specific in regard to the principle of inheritance. The Saints were commanded to purchase land for their inheritance as they participated in the movement of the gathering: "With one heart and with one mind, gather up your riches that ye may purchase an inheritance which shall hereafter be appointed unto you" (Doctrine and Covenants 45:12c). This indicates that individuals have the responsibility of acquiring sufficient resources with which to purchase their own inheritances. It also implies that there is to be some official recognition on the part of the church that such purchase is an inheritance (see also Doctrine and Covenants 48; 58:11). The law is clear also in respect to the fact that all inheritances are not alike, as evidenced by the right of choice apparently extended to Martin Harris: "Other directions . . . shall be given him of the Spirit, that he may receive his inheritance as seemeth him good" (Doctrine and Covenants 58:8a).

The acquisition of inheritances by the members of the church is a part of the gospel economy, as shown in the revelation given to Joseph Smith, Martin Harris, and others:

Wherefore a command I give unto them, that they shall not give these things unto the church, neither unto the world; nevertheless, inasmuch as they receive more than is needful for their necessities and their wants, it shall be given unto my storehouse, and the benefits shall be consecrated unto the inhabitants of Zion and unto their generations, inasmuch as they become heirs according to the laws of the kingdom . . . and for a reward of their diligence, and for their security for food and for raiment, for an inheritance.—Doctrine and Covenants 70:2a, b, 4a.

Provision for the storehouse contemplates broad coverage for meeting the needs of worthy members of the church:

Women have claim on their husbands for their maintenance until their husbands are taken; and if they are not found transgressors they shall have fellowship in the church; and if they are not faithful, they shall not have fellowship in the church; yet they may remain upon their inheritances according to the laws of the land.—82:1b.

The achievement of such a goal is, of course, dependent on the evolution of our society to a plane where surplus is equitably distributed and individuals are competent producers. This may seem impossible but it is nevertheless a goal of the church. This suggests, however, that inheritance is more than legal ownership, that it is not only the vesting of title in a person but that there is also recognition on the part of the church that the individual is morally and ethically as well as legally entitled to such.

The purpose of scripture is to show the way of life to those who seek after God. It seems important that every consideration be given to this principle of the law. Its application is basic to the welfare, economic success, and happiness of humanity.

I have heard some say that our whole philosophy is too complex and that it requires more than most people are willing to give by way of time, resources, and devotion. It does set up some standards that may seem beyond human achievement. One may evaluate what society has accomplished to date with what the goals and objectives of the church hold out as within the range of human achievement, and in the measuring of each find the answers to, "Is the building of the Zionic society within the range of our ability?" and "Is it worth the sacrifice that will be required?" Every person has to answer the questions personally. When I approached the problem of putting myself in the position of a believer in respect to the challenge, "Seek to bring forth and establish the Cause of Zion," I realized, to a considerable extent, that to many such seeking would appear more difficult than taking trips into outer space. I feel that explorations in Zion building will continue until we create the more perfect society, just as our exploration will continue until we find the source of life in the universe. Such efforts will ultimately blend in a search for God.

The revelation given through Joseph Smith III to the Reorganization challenged the members of the church to a higher form of community life—not isolation from others in the world but rather working with them. The revelation concerning it dealt with the need for mobilizing resources and personnel as well as recognizing the interdependence of all people of goodwill.

The Spirit saith further: That these organizations contemplated in the law may be effected and the benefits to be derived therefrom be enjoyed by the Saints, in such enjoyment they cannot withdraw themselves so completely from a qualified dependence upon their Gentile neighbors surrounding them as to be entirely free from intercommunication with them; yet it is incumbent upon the Saints while reaping the benefits of these organizations to so conduct themselves in the carrying into operation the details of their organizations as to be in the world but not of it, living and acting honestly and honorably before God and in the sight of all men, using the things of this world in the manner designed of God, that the places where they occupy may shine as Zion, the redeemed of the Lord.

The Bishop should be directed and authorized to proceed as soon as it shall be found practicable by consultation with the general authorities of the church who are made the proper counselors in spiritual and temporal things to carry out the provisions of the law of organization which are by the law made the duty of the Bishop.— 128:8a-c, 9.

Under the leadership of Joseph Smith III revelations regarding the work of the Bishopric in relation to the specifics of the latter-day movement were reaffirmed in Section 129:8:

The Spirit saith further: The attention of the church is called to the consideration of the revelation, given in answer to earnest application, with regard to temporal things. The word has been already given in agreement with revelations long since delivered to the church, that the temporalities of the church were to be under the charge and care of the Bishopric, men holding the office of bishop under a presiding head acting for the church in the gathering, caring for, and disbursing the contributions gathered from the Saints of moneys and properties under the terms of tithing, surplus, free-will offerings, and consecrations.

There has been consistency in the revelations received through Joseph Smith, Jr., Joseph Smith III, and subsequently relative to these principles delineated in Section 42 (previously referred to the constitutional law of the church).

Accounting, stewardship, agency, care of the poor, the gathering, inheritance, consecration, surplus, and storehouse all bear upon and have relation to the building of the Zionic community.

The Place of the Storehouse

The storehouse organization may establish factories, provide facilities of communication, transportation, production, financial institutions, and other essentials in the realm of economic affairs. Economic security, of course, should not become an end in itself, even though it is important. It should come as a result of proper attitude toward the organization of our economic affairs and their utilization.

The storehouse, which is under the direction and/or coordination of the Presiding Bishopric, may be organized in stakes where competent personnel is available to manage it. Decentralization of much of the economic and monetary affairs of the church is needed, and the storehouse can provide opportunity for men and women of required qualifications to serve the church as stewards in areas where members wish to further their economic interests through such a function.

The Storehouse

The storehouse need not be considered a mystery or something outside the scope of our needs. We become confused only when we try to make more of it than was intended. It is primarily an organization created within the provisions of civil law to meet the economic and monetary requirements of church members and groups. It requires the establishment of separate treasuries to receive funds consecrated by individuals and groups for either specific or general economic needs. It should not be confused with the General Fund treasury, which provides for the financial needs for the operation of the church in its educational, ministerial, and operational budgetary needs. The funds accruing to the storehouse arise out of the consecration of surplus by either individuals or groups, and surplus is of necessity made possible through the accumulation of property or wealth. *Unless there is increase, there can be no surplus; and if there is no surplus, there can be no storehouse.* Whether the surplus consists of money, goods, labor, or time is of relatively small importance. The principle is the same and may be so applied.

Surplus may provide for inheritances for the education of children, care of the aged and needy, or business capital. Work has been carried on for more than a decade to bring greater accord and understanding of procedures to be followed within the General Church and its stakes. A publication, *The Storehouse Principle and Its Implementation in the Stakes of Zion,** was developed in 1960 by a committee from the Order of Bishops; this had its genesis in the document approved by the World Conference of 1950 which the Order of Bishops asked me to develop relative to the function and purpose of the storehouse.

This publication contains an explanatory "Foreword":

Throughout its history as an organization the Reorganized Church of Jesus Christ of Latter Day Saints has been committed to the redemptive ministries of Zion. In economic terms such ministries involve procedures which have been traditionally described as the Storehouse, funded primarily by consecrations of surplus by individual stewards of the church.

Specific action looking toward the creation of the general Storehouse Treasury was taken by the World Conference of 1950 when a document prepared by Presiding Bishop G. L. DeLapp was approved. It had earlier been discussed by the First Presidency and Presiding Bishopric and approved by the Order of Bishops. One of the provisions of the 1950 document was that a procedure should be developed for guidance in the creation and operation of Stake Storehouses (GCR 977).

A committee of members of the Order of Bishops was appointed in 1960 by the Presiding Bishopric to study the purpose and function of storehouse principles and to recommend a point of beginning for storehouse functions within stakes. Those who have served in this capacity are: H. W. Cackler (chairman), L. W. Kohlman (secretary), L. R. Adams, J. E. Baldwin, F. C. Banta, T. A. Beck, W. C. Becker, J. H. Boren, E. C. Burdick, O. K. Byrn, J. A. Cadwell, H. S. Cash, Jr., C. D. Cederstrom, F. L. Dickson, H. T. Downey, H. P. Grundy, F. E. Hansen, E. T. Higdon, G. M. Hummel, A. C. Johnstone, L. E. Landsberg, R. E. Manuel, C. S. McArthur, H. J. Simons, W. E. Timms, and E. A. Theys.

Over a period of several years these men worked at their committee assignment in addition to their various ministerial and professional

*Available through Herald Publishing House

responsibilities. A voluminous research report was filed with the Presiding Bishopric, and a draft was produced for a *Constitution and Procedural Manual for Storehouse Operation in Stakes.*

After review and revisions of the draft this document is now presented as the basis for formal Storehouse organization in stakes. After experience has tested the principles and operational procedures, further refinements may be required. Meanwhile it is to be regarded as the official interpretation of the church law as it applies to the temporal functions of the Stake Storehouses. May the spirit of truth and revelation guide us in the creation of the resources of temporal Zionic ministries through its use.

In my opinion the production of this manual is one of the most important steps taken toward the implementation of the storehouse organization and other broad provisions of the law of temporalities which I have tried to delineate in this book. In it the basic law is succinctly stated, purposes are defined, and areas where it could be implemented listed. Uses of storehouse funds are clearly set forth as prescribed in the law. Functions of the storehouse are described in relation to both stakes and the General Church. The relationship of various funds such as oblation, agency, and surplus consecrations are also designated. The significance of the principle of inheritance and the function of stewardship associations becomes clearer as one studies this manual. For the first time in the history of the church the relationship of the use of temporalities to the establishment of Zion is matter-of-factly discussed; this is the result of many hours of research, quorum discussions, examination, and evaluation by those who have prayed for light for many years. It comes at a time of change and crisis both in respect to the future of the church and society. It remains for those of us who believe in the ultimate establishment of Zion to take heart, to prepare for changes which still loom ahead of us. Shall we lend our effort to the Cause of Zion, or shall we look upon the present and the future as some now describe it?

We have lived a delusion, we cannot know the world. Aided or unaided we stumble through an endless night, locked in a range of experience, the limits of which are given by what we are and where we live. Earth worm or dolphin, reaching our level of investigative competence, would find a different universe; and we ourselves, in the spiral galaxy of andromeda, would write different laws. Our eyes have seen the glory, but only within a narrow range, while by us, through us, flow visions for other eyes, music we shall never hear. We are a flicker of joy and grief and need, and shall not see the shores of this dark ocean. May we see but well enough to lay aside the weapons with which we are about to destroy, along with that little we do see, a potential of experience we know not of.—Allen Wheelis, *The End of the Modern Age,* page 115, Basic Books, Inc.

As members of the Church of Jesus Christ we too have walked through valleys of desolation, have climbed mountaintops to catch the vision of a new world, and have felt the presence of the guiding Spirit beckoning us toward Zionic community building. We have deplored the ruthlessness of our age, with its wars and savage struggle for political, economic, and even spiritual power. We have sensed through the revelatory processes evidenced in this church since its founding the immutability of divine laws: "I am come that they might have life, and that they might have it more abundantly" (John 10:10).

I, the Lord, stretched out the heavens, and builded the earth as a very handy work; and all things therein are mine; and it is my purpose to provide for my Saints, for all things are mine; but it must needs be done in mine own way.

These are not promises to just the few who may be fortunate enough to belong to the Restoration church; they are for men everywhere who heed the voice of Jesus Christ. But to the members of the Restoration church was given a special commission to carry the gospel of Jesus Christ to "all nations in every land ... that men of every tongue shall minister before me" (Doctrine and Covenants 116:1b).

The call to the church is to build the kingdom. Shall we do it? It has been in my mind for most of my life. Am I naïve to think that we or some other group will do it? I continue to say it will be done. Maybe I am like my father who worked daily with another man when I was in my late teens. Father used to tell me of his conversations with his fellow worker quite frequently. They were planting evergreens in Glenwood Park in Minneapolis. When payday came the other man looked forward to the fun he was going to have. Monday morning he would report to work with a headache and empty pockets. Once he said to my father, "You should enjoy life like I do. There is no life after death. When you're dead you're dead. I know you don't agree with me, but just suppose I am right. . . . Look at all the fun you have missed!" My father replied, "I have had an enjoyable weekend with my family and friends at church, and I have no headache. Suppose when you die you find that I am right. Who will be the best equipped to face that future?" With this he loaned the man money to tide him over until the next payday.

My desire to build the kingdom comes from some force within me and in relation to an impulsion from a Source greater than I. I prefer to try to the best of my ability, because history and all of man's experience points to the final consummation of God's purpose revealed through Jesus Christ.

Chapter 10

 APPROACHING THE ZIONIC COMMUNITY

The term Zion requires both definition and elaboration. It has been used to mean a *city* (Doctrine and Covenants 45:13; 100:5), a *people* (36:22; 99:11), and a *mode of life* (56:2; 102:2; Psalm 15).

Bishop J. A. Koehler, who wrote a great deal regarding the philosophy of Zion, once stated:

> Objective Zion is a group of people, a society, and may be located in any given place that is suited to its purposes. Subjective Zion is an ideal, a conception of life which appears in consciousness as worthy of contemplation and aspiration; a form of society considered subjectively.

Other Zionic concepts have been expressed in general terms—"Zion, the pure in heart"; "Zion, a social group of God's calling and choosing out of all eternity"; "Zion, a process of evolution—Zion, a reconstructed society"; "a new mode of life effected through social organization."

The Restoration concept of the Zionic community is varied to the extent that in each generation believers in Zion have been confronted with the changes in national and international relations, economic and social developments, educational and scientific advancement, health and welfare services, and burgeoning population in metropolitan centers.

The individual becomes less and less the master of his destiny. Often he is merely a statistic in a business or industrial conglomerate. He may even be a statistic in an organization supposedly concerned with the spiritual welfare of mankind, for there are those who would by persuasion or coercion force others to accept their prescribed theological beliefs. Such is usually premised on the leaders' belief in their own infallibility. In such cases these too become a part of the drive for social and economic power through the process of ex cathedra pronouncements. On the other hand, the clamor for individual recognition and personal identification is more prevalent than ever before; this is demonstrated in riots, strikes, and similar outbursts.

All I write is premised on the fact that the Restoration church holds out to mankind the promises and responsibilities available through the gift of "agency" (Doctrine and Covenants 36:7a; 90:5c; 98:10f).

The principle of agency is expressed in this statement which I made at the Business and Professional Men's Institute in February 1953:

> The Lord said unto Enoch, Behold these your brethren; they are the workmanship of my own hands, and I gave unto them their knowledge, in the day I created them; and in the Garden of Eden gave I unto man his agency. —36:7a, b.

This exercise of free agency is precious. We are ever free to associate ourselves together on a voluntary basis, engaging in those activities which are for the betterment of our social, economic, cultural, and spiritual welfare. There can be no fullness of spiritual welfare except as we are able to relate that which is temporal. The whole purpose of the temporal law is to give expression to the spiritual force and power resident within us. It is not to be done through coercion. It is not to be done because of fear, but because of our recognition of God and our belief in his Son, Jesus Christ, and because we wish to build the kingdom.

There is one thing I cherish in this church. It is the one thing above everything else that makes me adhere to its tenets and its doctrines and its philosophy. It is the right of agency—the right to express that which I think. However, the exercise of agency carries with it a corresponding responsibility to recognize and honor the rights of others.

Agency is one of the basics of Latter Day Saint philosophy. It is the right to choose in matters involving talents, capabilities, mental endowments, physical wealth and resources while recognizing God as Creator and Owner.

I have written in considerable detail of the principles on which the Restoration church was established. In this same vein I wish now to examine some of the goals of the church which have to do with a way of community life envisioned in the "cause of Zion."

The fact that America in 1830 was an agricultural nation may cause some to question the relation of land to a social program today. At that time land essential to a gathering movement was available. Today's highly industrialized society requires less land, and most people are not directly dependent on land holdings for a livelihood. Despite this, land has become unavailable to millions and its value more pronounced. Evidences of this are most obvious in over-populated areas.

Land often is acquired by the thousands of acres or in tracts for industrial and commercial purposes by great conglomerates while thousands of individuals lack the means to buy even a small lot. This is unfortunate because land ownership provides a sense of security; without it there is frequently social unrest. Thus, it is important for those of us who believe in the gathering to consider the place of land in the Zionic program.

There is a definite relationship between the function of the storehouse and land acquisition and usage. This was established in the Restoration preceding 1844 and reaffirmed as a policy in the Reorganization.[1] The storehouse serves as a primary agency in the purchase of lands; however this is not the only function of the storehouse,[2] nor is the purchase of land limited to the storehouse. Land purchase has been accomplished through the use of other funds such as the Ministerial Reserve Fund which was established in keeping with the principle of storehouse organization and function.

The financial policy was developed in 1931 and approved by the General Conference of 1932. At that time all lands owned by the church were encumbered with mortgage indentures. The most difficult situation confronting the church at that time was the blanket indenture which hypothecated all church properties as collateral to the mortgage of $335,000 on the Auditorium. Hence all church debt had to be paid off before there could be freedom of use of the land owned by the church or completion of the Auditorium.

Several stewardship programs had been initiated: The Holden Development Association, organized to hold title to lands at Atherton, Missouri, to be used in a farming and chicken-raising undertaking and the Spring Branch farms, six miles east of Independence along the Little Blue River. This and several other projects were unsuccessful due to debt restrictions and general economic conditions. It was deemed advisable to discontinue such enterprises until the debt was paid, because little assurance could be given to those willing to participate that clear title could be obtained.

The church lands were subsequently cleared of all encumbrance with the payment of existing mortgages and the indebtedness against the Auditorium. Throughout the years until 1966 additional lands were purchased which, with those originally held, amounted to the present figure of over 8,000 acres.

All proposed purchases were evaluated and appraised on

the basis of their contiguity to property already owned by the church and their agricultural productivity. (Studies made at different times relative to land ownership and usage are available.[3]) In addition, there was the possibility of such land being used in the development of a Zionic community or communities.

As the church faces the future in respect to such projects, a tremendous challenge thrusts itself into the thinking of all members who look forward to the actual establishment of Zion as well as the development of theoretical and philosophical concepts.

Throughout the years I have recognized that there must be not only the vision but also an understanding of what is involved in the development of techniques, structure, organization, and facilities essential to successful community building.

In seeking such knowledge I have found it helpful to participate in various municipal projects. From such experience I have learned that the task of building a Zionic community could well take two or three generations. Many more church members will need similar participation and experience if we are to succeed. Gaining such experience for most people will be an extracurricular obligation. Few are inclined to give the hours necessary to serve on a commission that brings little if any compensation. Such service requires devotion to a cause beyond the realm of remuneration. The cause for us is Zion.

When I speak of land I refer not only to agricultural or industrial holdings but land for world headquarters needs, church buildings throughout the world. Purchases made by the Bishopric with the approval of the First Presidency and other responsible church officers have added to our holdings around the Independence Sanitarium and Hospital and Resthaven.

At the request of the Presiding Bishopric a very capable and devoted church man gave many hours of his time to the contacting and following through with persons owning land in the headquarters area; this resulted in the purchase of over seventy-five pieces of property which otherwise might not have been acquired or, because of delays in acquisition, would have been much more costly.

Justification for land purchase is obvious when one sees the problems existing in society today. It is for the alleviation of these that the church is called to establish a better type of community life. Once when I was serving as foreman of the county grand jury I went to lunch with the county prosecutor. While talking about the steady increase in crime he said, with a sense of frustration, "It takes a mile of effort to make an inch of progress." The least we can do is work for that one inch.

New communities are being built—and others in the planning stage—that are designed to promote better social relationships. These need to be looked at, studied, and analyzed. Such communities range from New Columbia, Maryland, to Winnebago, Missouri. Their objectives, costs, and results should be evaluated in the light of present social needs, but—even more important—this should be done in relation to what we as a church conceive to be the function of the community.

In 1969 planners of the Professional and Vocational Associations Conference met after several months of preparation to establish conference goals. These were outlined in the keynote address by Dr. John A. Smith:

1. Conduct an in-depth study of the city of Independence, its resources, needs, and people.
2. Evaluate its place in the metropolitan area economically, socially, and educationally.
3. Consider the Center City's future in relation to the gathering, as

to industrial development, employment opportunities, and education facilities.

4. Stimulate professional-vocational interaction in community design for the Center City and consider the application of these principles in other communities.

5. Seek skilled participation in total stewardship toward Restoration goals, a community building process, by consecrated professional-vocational people.

The work of the conference was covered in a brochure titled, *Skilled Participation in Community Programs.*[4] This included some sixteen reports from the associations and was climaxed by a resolution "to establish a research organization." This has been established and has moved slowly but surely toward goals comparable to those outlined. It is now functioning in the field of community research, and I feel that progress toward some of the objectives of Zion will be dependent on and related to the work of this organization. It needs the support of individual members of the church; this support will make a sustained contribution to the cause of Zion. Through such endeavors we shall learn how to be "in the world" and to lift the standards of community life to a position that will fulfill the commandment in Doctrine and Covenants 129:8:

The Spirit saith further: The attention of the church is called to the consideration of the revelation, given in answer to earnest supplication, with regard to temporal things. The word has been already given in agreement with revelations long since delivered to the church, that the temporalities of the church were to be under the charge and care of the Bishopric, men holding the office of bishop under a presiding head acting for the church in the gathering, caring for, and disbursing the contributions gathered from the Saints of moneys and properties under the terms of tithing, surplus, free-will offerings, and consecrations. The word which has been given at a late period should not have been so soon forgotten and disregarded by the church or any of its members. "I am God; I change not" has been known to the church and the eldership since the coming of the angel with the message

221

of restoration. Under it the church has sought the Lord and received from time to time that which was deemed sufficient for the time to govern the church and its ministers, both of the spiritual and the temporal divisions of the work. The church has been directed to accede to the rendition of the Bishopric with respect to the temporal law; and until such heed is paid to the word which has been given, and which is in accordance with other revelations given to the church, which had been before given, the church can not receive and enjoy the blessings which have been looked for when Zion should be fully redeemed. Therefore, hearken once again unto the voice of inspiration, in warning and instruction, and conform to that which is given and receive what is awaiting the upright and the pure in heart.

New Communities

Community building has been an objective of the church since its very beginning: "Monday, June 24 (1833) there was a conference of the elders held at Westfield, when the following plat of the City of Zion was adopted and ordered sent to the brethren in Zion" (Church History, Volume 1, page 297).

Records indicate that careful planning had been given to the laying out of the City of Zion; unfortunately it was never carried out. The plans for Kirtland and Nauvoo also bear evidence of the vision and ability of those who were seeking to build new communities, but these experiments were realized only in part.

In keeping with tradition and the law, community building continues to motivate the Saints. There are, however, many problems pertaining to community building today that did not exist in the 1830's. This is particularly true in the central areas. Sewage disposal, for example, was not a major problem in the development of the West. Water was obtained from wells or streams and rivers. Electric power was unknown. Community planning was usually quite casual in the early years of America's development. Those who laid out cities in those days were largely concerned with business centers, residential areas, wide streets, and public buildings that would meet the needs of the community. Today's planning is a very complex and costly procedure—far beyond anything that was contemplated in the days of the coming forth of the Restoration church.

In the central area community planning has taken on some highly interesting aspects. An organization called the Mid-America Regional Council (MARC) is responsible for much of the coordinating. Also located in Kansas City is the Institute for Community Studies Organization, composed of a highly trained staff with broad experience in the technical, sociological, and physical needs of communities.

A most important development resulting from the work of Community Studies was the organization of the Metropolitan Area Planning Council some years ago. This was formed primarily to bring about a coordination of the civic and municipal interests of all citizens and corporate bodies within the six-county area to avoid duplication of sewage lines, water facilities, power plants and, in fact, all utilities.

Organizations such as these do much to stimulate civic interest but often serve only briefly because of a lack of follow-through. The objectives, however, are frequently sought by succeeding groups, and progress continues to be made. Particularly is this true when organizations (such as MARC) provide representation from all towns and political subdivisions of the area.

Regional Health and Welfare Council

Along with the development of the councils previously mentioned a Regional Health and Welfare Council has been developed which covers the same six-county area. Its purposes are set forth in its bylaws, from which I quote:

To promote, by study, planning and stimulation of others, a proper balance of civic, health and welfare services, within the broad sense of those terms, in the metropolitan area of Greater Kansas City;

To encourage individuals and groups to work together on community problems and to mobilize the community-wide support behind needed development or changes in community civic, health and welfare projects and services;

To advance the use of community resources in providing civic, health and welfare services. . . .

Other organizations which mobilize and coordinate separate agencies are the United Funds and the Kansas City Area Hospital Association.

Philanthropic trusts and foundations have been largely instrumental in providing funds for the initial and sometimes sustaining work of these educational and charitable organizations.

In addition to the foregoing, organizations have also been created by businessmen to bring industry to the Greater Kansas City area. Similar organizations have been formed in Independence.

For a number of years the Midwest Research Group has been functioning in the Greater Kansas City Area serving industry and business in the development of new products. This organization has scientists, engineers, and technicians qualified to tackle almost any problem of industrial, community development.

I mention these organizations to give some understanding of the problems involved in community planning, the methods used, and the objectives attainable. It is for those of us who are church members to relate our own ideals, ideas, and objectives to the common goals of the community as a whole and to integrate our interests with those of an expanding community.

When I review conditions at the time the revelations were

given to the church which pointed to Independence as the Center Place I realize that the country was undeveloped and the population very small; yet the revelations pertaining to social progress and economic organization were forward-looking in concept and far-reaching in implication. Today we must think of community building in much broader terms than did the members of the early church, and we must go even beyond the concepts which many of our church people have developed through the last few decades.

We can make our best contribution only if we understand the problems involved in present community building. The type of planning being carried on in the Center Place is certainly essential.

I do not think it is too far-fetched to think that with the growth of our church we could do some experimental work in community building on a small scale. (By "small" I mean in comparison with what is being undertaken in some of the metropolitan areas; yet we must still think in terms of millions of dollars.)

The growth of Independence in the last two decades has required the development and expansion of its electric power plant. The 1972 annual report showed continuing growth. Assets for that year increased in the amount of $4,701,015, bringing total assets to the amount of $47,506,583. Net assets over bonded indebtedness amounted to $23,346,918. The municipally-owned plant has an excellent record of efficient management throughout its history.

The Independence water plant is owned privately by the Mott Foundation and has a record of reinvesting all profits in the improvement and expansion of its plant and lines. Additions since 1963 to pumping and treatment facilities, reservoirs, transmission mains, etc., amounted to $4,896,464. This too has been the result of consistently having good management and interest in the community at top levels.

We need to do some research in relating the program of the church to the all-important task of community planning and building. We must study our own problems and evaluate our opportunities in the light of present needs, while at the same time trying to foresee what the needs of the expanding community will be.

Housing, an Essential in Community Building

Providing suitable housing for families is a continuing problem. An account of the development of government housing is given in an article "Government Housing Activities" by E. Everett Ashley III in the *Harvard Business Review,* Volume 19, No. 2. In it the author points out that government action began in 1932, and that subsequently a great deal of legislation was enacted which resulted in the setting up of such agencies as the Reconstruction Finance Corporation, Federal Home Loan Banks, Home Owners' Loan Corporation, Federal Savings and Loan Associations, and—most successful of all—the Federal Housing Administration. The purpose of such legislation was to make finances available on terms that could be met by the average wage earner wanting to own a home.

The Theory of Community Building Explored

Building a community requires adequate land areas, public utilities (telephone, electric, water and sewage systems), sidewalks, roads, parkways, transportation facilities (bus systems, airports, railroads), business and industry, housing, public buildings, schools, and people who are qualified to function in responsibilities of community life.

If we are to build a new community, more land will have to be acquired. If we pursue the policy of locating individual families in already established areas, the need for purchasing additional acreage will vary according to the type of community, the number of members already located there, and the training of individuals to fit into positions of responsibility. They should be encouraged to invest their own capital and thus make capital acquired through other sources available for further expansion. In any event, sufficient land would need to be purchased and consolidated to assure reasonable success in providing vocational opportunities for the development of nuclei around which to build.

In the building of a new community, we must consider many factors—costs, methods of financing, relationship of the individual to the community, services each is to perform and benefits each is to receive. A form of government or of rules to govern community relationship must be established. The type of people composing the community and the basis of selection must also be worked out. The question, "What advantages will be obtained?" may well be asked. Can we have reasonable assurance that a community so established will have permanence? Will it provide a better way of life? How will members of the community earn a livelihood? These questions are not easily answered, but the attempt must be made.

Changing Times

Changing conditions are reflected in the movement of families to the suburbs of large cities, leaving the central areas of the cities to deteriorate. As a church, we need to think in terms of all the changes which are taking place. It would seem that we could start on a very small basis as a satellite community close to some large city which would provide opportunity for a diversity of employment.

The geographical and population limit of cities is controlled by two factors: the financial ability to provide improvements and the distance from profitable occupation and employment. Planning would require the development of a land-use map showing industry, railroad, and commercial areas as well as multiple-dwelling, two-family, and single-family housing divisions.

In discussing "Urban Land Uses" in the *Harvard City Planning Studies* (Volume 4), Bartholomew points out:

> Cities are divided into two distinct types—self-contained and satellite. The self-contained municipalities are those which are totally self-sufficient, at least as to all the facilities and services necessary for complete urban existence. Satellite cities are those which are contiguous to larger municipalities and which are dependent upon the parent city not only for their initial development but also for their continued existence.

Our planning should also include consideration of the amount of property that could be developed immediately or in the near future; the extent to which unused property could be purchased and retained without use; and areas to be developed for public, semi-public, and private purposes.

One of the most stimulating books I have read is Frank Lloyd Wright's *Living City*. In it he declares that decentralization is imperative. He pictures small cities utilizing the vast spaces that are still open. Here there will be one acre per person; soot and smoke will be eliminated; resources will be mobilized to purchase materials for building; and men may help in part or altogether in the building of their houses. He points out that public transportation can make possible the overcoming of the handicaps of distance between communities. He envisions towns with one or two skyscrapers instead of many. Agriculture may be the pursuit of more—rather than fewer—people. And he declares that safety is no longer to be found in fortifications:

> Fortifications, that once upon a time protected the might of the baron on his feudal estate, in our day can no longer fortify. As homes, fortifications are dead.

Modern America needs no longer to box up or hole up for

protection, or dive into a burrow in any city. Instead security in every sense is best found in the wide free spacing and integral construction, the spiritual perception of what we are calling decentralization. Spaciousness is for safety as well as beauty.—*Living City*, page 96.

As a church we find ourselves in an entirely different world from that which existed under the leadership of Joseph Smith, Jr. The principles of social living were enunciated in the revelations given through him to the church. It is for us, in our planning, to familiarize ourselves with developments and to relate them to the fundamental principles given to guide us in the establishment of Zion.

Despite the complexity of our present world, we must try to accomplish the goal set out by Carver in his book, *The Essential Factors of Social Evolution,* in which he states:

They who can be in the world but not of it, who can keep themselves unspotted from the world, who in the midst of demoralizing influences of modern civilization, with its great cities, can remain immune to their contagion, are to survive, reproduce their kind, and build a civilization for the future.

The building of a community is not an impossibility. Large areas of land are still available in the stakes surrounding the Center Place. The mobilization of manpower and resources, while a tremendous challenge, is in keeping with the goals to which we are commissioned. Helping to rebuild existing cities and taking our places where we live, while planning for the community of tomorrow, should make life worthwhile.

For those of us committed to the Zionic concept, I wish to refer to Doctrine and Covenants 42 to give emphasis to the goals of the church. I shall not attempt to delineate all the contents of that revelation, but I do want to point out that the goals cover a broad program of individual challenges and collective objectives, ranging all the way from observing personal stewardship to establishing the storehouse and building a Zionic community.

Section 42 was accepted as a guideline by the Reorganization in 1860. Joseph Smith III proved himself to be both prophet and statesman as he assumed leadership of the church after the breakup following his father's death. In 1894 he received a revelation (Section 122) which reaffirmed the divinity of the revelation given in Section 42:

> The Spirit saith unto you, that "with the Lord one day is as a thousand years, and a thousand years as a day"; therefore, the law given to the church in Section 42, over the meaning of some parts of which there has been so much controversy, is as if it were given today.— 122:6a, b.

I have previously stated my thinking about the continuity of revelatory processes. I feel that no man has a complete knowledge of the scriptures, and I readily admit my own lack, but it has been my experience in reading and evaluating to form a philosophy predicated on the teachings of Jesus Christ, the Old Testament, and the Book of Mormon. This philosophy helps me to maintain a faith in the ultimate accomplishment of God's purpose for mankind—the building of the kingdom.

All civilizations have at times moved toward world brotherhood as the hoped-for solution to society's problems. W. Louis Wagar writes:

> Seized by an exhausting anxiety, twentieth-century man has lost his sense of direction. Scaling the heights of power only made him dizzy. "Everything," says Erich Kahler, "is in a state of flux, everything is open to question, everything is involved in perpetual change and dissolution." Paul Tillich compares anxiety now universal in western civilization with the mental climate of Europe during the decline and fall of Rome and the waning of the middle ages. But the twentieth century confronts humanity with the most radical crisis in history; and the responsibility is man's alone.[5]

Further defining his purpose Wagar says:

This, then, is a study of the search for a philosophy of world order in recent thought. If the search is ultimately successful, it will supply coming generations with a life-orienting and life-fulfilling objective in an age staggered by confusion. And before time runs out for mankind, men may succeed in passing from the sphere of thought to the sphere of concrete practical action. . . .

A word of explanation. An organic world civilization is not a Utopia, nor do any of the prophets surveyed in this book so regard it. It will be a world of finite men and women, no less corruptible than the men and women of Imperial Rome. . . . But it must be a flourishing concern, a business in full operation, able to minister to the needs of all men, able to respond flexibly to new crises. . . . It is the best form of life possible for mankind in an age of unlimited technics and a world community of peril. . . .

Wagar presents a picture which has a degree of realism in it, but it is difficult for me to conceive of a world brotherhood based purely on the technics of our present society. While there are many men in business, finance, industry, politics, government, and the professions who are highly moral, present trends of our social and economic society seem to refute the possibility of a brotherhood without a spiritual and religious base. Such a base can be developed only when there is a blending of the spiritual and temporal. This is what latter-day revelation calls for.

Wagar undoubtedly has doubts about this too, for he raises the question, "Can men, remaining men, always through bluff or diplomacy or good sense somehow manage to avoid Armageddon?" He discusses the possibility of a world government, the problems of "intellectual, spiritual, economic and political integration." Covering the points of view of various scholars, he points out that some believe in the existence of a higher realm.

It will not, of course be man's last great experience. Toynbee does believe in the existence of a higher realm of being in cosmos, and man's supreme task is to achieve communion with it. But this does not absolve him of his terrestrial responsibilities.[6]

Hocking concedes to Toynbee the existence of isolable phenomena in history such as "civilizations" and a certain historic rhythm of rise and fall. Civilizations generate their own poisons; they cannot exist intact forever. Nonetheless, "some human achievements stay achieved, though their significance is continually revised by the emergence of novelty around them." As a whole, history does not repeat itself. Civilizations do not perish entirely.

But Jasper nourishes no high optimism about the human prospect. We live in a world of despiritualized masses who have sold their freedom for soulless comfort and hollow security, and we live in a world under the shadow of the threat of nuclear annihilation. . . .[7]

Many people have written of their thoughts, ideas, and anticipations of world order. Wagar lists quite a number, including specialists in history, philosophy, sociology, and the humanities. Some have written hopefully, but they are in the minority. More are inclined to view the future with pessimism.

Looking back, Wagar says:

The last safe chance to impose order on the planet by force was lost in the late 1940's by the United States, and such chance may never come again.

For this is rapidly becoming a world without truth, not without practical truths, handy for solving immediate, everyday problems. What mid-century man lacks is utter truth. The whole avant-garde in theology, philosophy, and science assures him that if he thinks he sees the utter truth, he sees only a mirage.[8]

He presents ideas of others and comments on their wisdom, their great "breadth of mind, their staggering rendition," but he also perceives that each one gives only a "specialized, personalized glimpse of truth too fuzzy and incomplete to ever be represented as the real thing."[9]

In his last chapter he restates his faith.

The human race may go on, if it wills well enough, for thousands of millions of years. In all this fullness of time, with a cosmos to explore gigantic beyond belief, much more is in store than another round of cold war crises or the synthesis of the species in a world civilization. A few alternatives and further possibilities spring to mind, at the deep end of time.[10]

In a pessimistic volume *The End of the Modern Age* (Basic Books, Inc., New York-London, 1970) Allen Wheelis discusses the character of the present. He begins by saying, "The age is ending, the house is coming down—all the rafters, all the towers, all the clocks. It was built of a dream. The dream closes."

He recalls the remarkable beginning of science and the resistance of the church to it: "In the middle ages reason is in the shadow of God, subject to curtailment and veto; God acting through his deputies on earth is the final authority."[11]

Then he discusses progress: "In the modern age the world becomes an independent and self-sufficient mechanism."[12]

He closes his book with a flicker of hope despite the possible hazards of the future:

We have lived a delusion, we cannot know the world. Aided or unaided we stumble through the endless night, locked in a range of experience the limits of which are given by what we are and where we live. Earthworm or dolphin, reaching our level of investigative competence, would find a different universe; and we ourselves, in the spiral galaxy of Andromeda, would write different laws. Our eyes have seen the glory, but only within a narrow range, while by us, through us, flow visions for other eyes, music we shall never hear. We are a flicker of joy and grief and need, and shall not see the shores of this dark ocean. May we see but well enough to lay aside the weapons with which we are about to destroy, along with the little we do see, a potential of experience we know not of.

Joseph Smith, Jr., through the gift of revelation, also was able to look beyond the present:

And worlds without number have I created, and I also created

233

them for mine own purpose; and by the Son I created them, which is mine Only Begotten. And the first man of all men have I called Adam, which is many. But only an account of this earth, and the inhabitants thereof, give I unto you; for behold there are many worlds which have passed away by the word of my power; and there are many also which now stand, and numberless are they unto man; but all things are numbered unto me; for they are mine, and I know them. [13]

It is important that we see clearly our relationship to God and the world we live in, and that we learn to appreciate the knowledge made available to us by many minds from both the past and the present.

Some scholars have studied the influence of industrial and technical developments on society. John Kenneth Galbraith in his book *The New Industrial State* refers to the rise of the modern corporation. In a short chapter he reviews the days when business was largely the product of entrepreneurs. Now the individual seldom operates in this fashion. Galbraith describes the development of management as follows:

With the rise of the modern corporation, the emergence of the organization required by modern technology and planning, and the divorce of the owner of the capital from control of the enterprize, the entrepreneur no longer exists as an individual person in the mature industrial enterprize. Everyday discourse, except in the economics textbooks, recognizes this change. It replaces the entrepreneur as the directing force of the enterprize, with management. This is a collective and imperfectly defined entity; in the large corporation it embraces chairman, president, those vice-presidents with important staff or departmental responsibility, occupants of other major staff positions and, perhaps, division or department heads not included above. It includes, however, only a small proportion of those who, as participants, contribute information to group decisions. This latter group is very large; it extends from the most senior officials of the corporation to where it meets, at the outer perimeter, the white and blue collar workers whose function is to conform more or less mechanically to instruction or routine. It embraces all who bring specialized knowledge, talent or experience to group decision-making. This, not the management, is the guiding intelligence—the brain—of the enterprize. There is no name for all who participate in group decision-making or the organization which they form. I propose to call this organization the Technostructure.... He [the entrepreneur] is still, of course, to be found in smaller firms and in larger ones that have yet to reach full maturity of organization.[14]

This clearly represents what is taking place in the United States and undoubtedly has its counterpart in some of the large corporations which have established branches in other countries. The combined resources of the major companies wield a tremendous influence in all fields. Will such a system hold up under the present trend for increased recognition of the individual? I believe that the technostructure will take on more power in all areas of social endeavor. Management groups already play an important role in both secular and religious organizations. This results in the separation of the individual from management, and the goals of society may become lost in the interest of those in control of the enterprise. America was built on the foundation of individual rights and responsibilities. The same principle applies to the church. Yet the growing technostructure may become the world order which many advocate. There was a time when monopolies were fought bitterly, but today there is a tremendous increase in conglomerates. Small companies are absorbed, strengthened, or dissolved according to the decisions of management groups, and often with little consideration for stockholders.

Galbraith, writing of the future of the industrial system, points out its dangers as well as its potential for good:

If we continue to believe that the goals of the industrial system—the expansion of output, the companion increase in consumption, technological advance, the public images that sustain it—are coordinate with life, then all of our lives will be in the service of these

235

goals. What is consistent with these ends we shall have or be allowed; all else will be off limits. . . .

If, on the other hand, the industrial system is only a part and relatively a diminished part, of life, there is much less concern. Aesthetic goals will have price of place; those who serve them will not be subject to the goals of the industrial system; the industrial system itself will be subordinate to the claims of these dimensions of life. . . .

If other goals are strongly asserted, the industrial system will fall into its place as a detached and autonomous arm of the state, but responsive to the larger purposes of the society.

We have seen wherein the chance for salvation lies. The industrial system, in contrast with its economic antecedents, is intellectually demanding. It brings into existence, to serve its intellectual and scientific needs, the community that hopefully will reject its monopoly of social purpose.[15]

The preceding quotes set forth quite succinctly the potential purpose, goals, and ultimate benefits of the industrial system—provided society will give proper direction to its further growth and the utilization of its resources for the attainment of higher objectives. Can this be achieved? It is indeed a difficult question to answer; particularly when we see on every hand the markets, discount houses, automobile factories, and other manufacturing and retail establishments of our country that have burgeoned in numbers and in the variety of products in the last few decades.

When we examine the philosophy of "needs and just wants," we are overwhelmed with the magnitude of the task of educational enlightenment and stewardship discipline with which we are confronted. Fortunately we are not the only ones recognizing the trends and dangers ahead. Affluence in the United States and other countries may soon exhaust itself in the production of unneeded goods; this is socially criminal when viewed in the light of millions of impoverished people who lack shelter, food, and clothing.

We must continue our endeavors to implement the Zionic

community organization to which the church is committed. This will not be easily achieved. The industrial age is not the product of just a few years. James Morris in his book *The Road to Huddersfield* takes the reader with him on a journey to five continents in which he begins at the village of Huddersfield, England:

Crouched in a declivity among the Yorkshire Moors, in the harsh allure of the Bronte Country, there lies the town of Huddersfield: and in that foursquare earthly English borough, a place of drab and fusty reputation, this book properly and symbolically begins. It is not guides or hotel reservations that you will need if ever you make the pilgrimage to those stark smoke-filled valleys, but a responsive sense of history, for Huddersfield's fascination is more evocative than architectural: her passport to Baedeker is the fact that here in those grim moorlands of northern England the technical revolution began—a historical convulsion so fierce and inflammatory that it has changed half the world already and is now tumultuously transforming the rest.

Then he describes the town as it is today:

All around you, as you stand at the top of Chapel Hill, you may see the monuments of that tremendous but brutal event which erupted among the Yorkshire hill farms a couple of centuries ago: the long huddle of the textile mills, creeping away to the moor's edge; the marching file of tall brick chimneys, their vapors drifting into the dusk; the coveys of cramped terrace houses, jammed hugger-mugger against the hillsides; the dingy red brick everywhere, the patina of dirt, labor, and middle age. It is not at first sight an exuberant scene.... Here, nevertheless, in the Huddersfields of the north our modern world was born.

Morris continues his description of that portion of England and goes on to report of the growth of the industrial development in other countries, the resultant conditions which industry created, and the disparities between rich and poor.

The Huddersfields were the pace-makers, but today there is

237

scarcely a nation in the world that does not wish to follow them down the highway to the mills. . . .

The simpler half of our contemporary world, then, with its eyes on rockets and refrigerators of the sophisticated half, is hoping to modernize itself; and indeed, by and large the difference between a rich nation and a poor one is the difference between a mechanical and a muscular society.

He goes on to discuss the outreach of the Russians and the insatiable demand from underprivileged nations for money from them and the affluent West.

This competitive benevolence is today's most powerful instrument for hastening the universal technical revolution, for transplanting in the poor world the mechanical civilization that Russians and Americans willy-nilly share.

This book is a story of the World Bank and its operations in five continents. Morris gives a vivid description of peoples and places and social conditions and tells how the World Bank functions to meet some of the needs.

An evaluation of all that was done through the World Bank would be difficult to make, but Morris closes his book on a reasonably optimistic note. Of Huddersfield he says:

She is shabby still, but not heartless, for she has virtually eliminated poverty and illiteracy. She is a town rich in choral societies and brass bands, the Invalid Tricycle Club, the Rough Stuff Fellowship, the noisy young Luddites on their motorcycles. . . . She is, in short, no longer an exciting or a provocative place, but she has evolved a society that is, as human institutions go, strong, decent, and kindly.

The cause of Zion is a challenge to the believer both in the present and future. With all the technical and scientific advancement made in recent decades there is increased need for a blending of spiritual motivation through the sublimation of that which is material. We are reminded of this relationship in the revelation given to the church in 1830: "Wherefore, verily I say unto you, that all things unto me are spiritual, and not at any time have I given unto you a law which was temporal, neither any man, nor the children of men" (Doctrine and Covenants 28:9a).

This holds true when we consider the life and building of the community. It must take form in the minds of men before it can be transformed into selected land areas, streets, buildings, institutions, and facilities.

The rhythm of life in cities seems to be an alternation between materialization: the concrete structure, detaching itself through a human response, takes on a symbolic meaning, uniting the knower and the known; while subjective images, ideas, intuitions, only partly formed in their original expression, likewise take on material attributes, in visible structures, whose very size, position, complexity, organization, and esthetic form extend the area of meaning and value, otherwise inexpressible. City design is thus the culminating point of a socially adequate process of materialization.[16]

Some people feel that cities are the concretion of the ideas and ideals that make for abundant living. Throughout the ages they have served as places of refuge against invaders, as centers of economic organization and development, as providers of religious and educational institutions, and as institutional resources which could best provide for the needs of man.

As I have stated and restated in my work as a bishop, the message of the Restoration is an all-inclusive commission to preach the gospel in its fullness. This centers in the life and ministry of Jesus Christ and comprehends the establishment of a society equipped with the basic essentials to creatively provide for the needs of its members in all regards, ranging from the basic necessities of life to the overall educational, spiritual, and social ministries conducive to the complete development of human personality.

As a church we have not dedicated ourselves sufficiently to this task. We have been satisfied at times just to be "in the world." Now we have reached a point where, if we are to survive as a church, we must fulfill the rest of that commitment which would provide through stewardship organizations and associations the vehicle for carrying forward the Zionic movement:

> It is incumbent upon the Saints while reaping the benefits of these organizations to so conduct themselves in the carrying into operation the details of their organizations as to be in the world but not of it, living and acting honestly and honorably before God and in the sight of all men, using the things of this world in the manner designed of God, that the places where they occupy may shine as Zion, the redeemed of the Lord.—Doctrine and Covenants 128:8b, c.

New Communities

Despite our desire to build better communities we often have been slow in sensing the need for participation in improvement projects. Today, more than ever before, concerned people are organizing groups to study and analyze social problems. As a result new communities are emerging— some well planned, some highly experimental. One of the most successful is Columbia, Maryland, the story of which is told by Gurney Breckenfield in his book, *Columbia and the New Cities.* The history of the planning, financing, and building of this city is fascinating. The first step was in acquiring and consolidating land areas adequate for a community.

> Through the summer and into the fall of 1963 a mystery perplexed the 53,000 inhabitants of Howard County, Maryland. Somebody, or perhaps several somebodies, were buying up a vast amount of farm and woodland in their midst, and the operation was being conducted in particularly secretive fashion.[17]

The building of the city was a tremendous task, but because it was well planned and organized, it was a success. Provision was made for every conceivable need from single-family houses to apartments and townhouses, diversified employment, neighborhood schools, shopping centers, well laid-out streets and boulevards, and contiguity to major highways.

In pursuit of his Promethean objective, Rouse* combines the zeal of a missionary, the vision of a prophet, and the icy calculation of a cost accountant. The surest way to make the American City what it ought to be, he says, is to demonstrate that it is enormously profitable to do it a better way.... Columbia's innovations—and its exemplary triumphs—lie in urban sociology.[18]

Other matters discussed in the book are the development of industry, diversity in population, and essential ingredients of a great community.

Other new towns, both in America and abroad, also are described by Breckenfield. For those of us who believe in the Zionic movement there is need for much study and research relative to community building.

Sporadic attempts have been made at different times by the church. The early days at Kirtland, Independence, Nauvoo, Far West, and Lamoni revealed the interest on the part of church leaders and members. That interest has never died and the commission to gather has never been revoked. In more recent years a number of projects have been undertaken. The Atherton venture was incomplete because of the depression of the 1930's. A few groups have had a degree of success. The Bellevista Subdivision, for example, has served a basic need, both by way of experience for those who developed it and as a residential area for a number of church families.

---

*Mortgage banker and civic leader.

1. Doctrine and Covenants 42:9; 122:6.
2. *The Storehouse Principle and Its Implementation in the Stakes* (brochure), Herald Publishing House, 1971.
3. See "Land Survey—August 1959" by Bert Johnson. Copies available from Zionic Research Office and Office of the Presiding Bishopric.
4. May be available at Zionic Research Institute Office.
5. W. Louis Wagar, *The City of Man, Prophecies of a World Civilization in Twentieth Century Thought,* Houghton Mifflin Company, Boston; Riverside Press, Cambridge, page 3 of Introduction.
6. *Ibid.,* page 91.
7. *Ibid.,* page 105.
8. *Ibid.,* pages 240-42.
9. *Ibid.,* page 241.
10. *Ibid.,* page 262.
11. *The End of the Modern Age,* Basic Books, Inc., 1970, New York-London, page 16.
12. *Ibid.,* page 114.
13. Doctrine and Covenants 22:21b-e.
14. John Kenneth Galbraith, *The New Industrial State,* Houghton Mifflin, page 71.
15. *Ibid.,* pages 398-399.
16. Lewis Mumford, *The City in History*, Harcourt, Brace and World, New York, page 113.
17. *Columbia and the New Cities,* Washburn, Ives, Inc., New York, page 168.
18. *Ibid.,* page 172.

Chapter 11

SOCIAL PLANNING—
OLD AND NEW COMMUNITIES

Social planning in recent years has taken on a new dimension. This applies to both old, established communities and new ones being built. The Kansas City Institute for Community Studies, in a March 1969 report, outlined the purpose of a preliminary study (based on health and social welfare work in Pittsburgh and Allegheny County, Pennsylvania):

To lay the groundwork for the reappraisal and redevelopment project and to develop recommendations for further steps to be taken by the association in the interest of improving the effectiveness of its own program as well as those of other community agencies. Such review shall take account but not be limited to the following:

a. The present range of health, education and welfare services; the governmental and voluntary structure for raising the money required, the development of efficient ways of delivering health and welfare services, the distribution of funds for services promised; and the regulation of the demand for funds to continue activities and to establish new ones.

b. The research and planning resources currently available, such as the Health and Welfare Association, other voluntary bodies, the governmental agencies at various levels, the colleges and universities, and the ways such organizations relate to one another.

Some of the recommendations in the report were as follows:

We recommend that there be created a Citizens Conference to monitor on a continuing basis the community welfare services system of the Greater Pittsburgh Area and to bring maximum public exposure to the alternative choices available in policies and programming.

Papers written by specialists in various fields were made a part of the report. These covered governmental services, citizen participation, manpower, the black community, health, welfare, and education. Such a comprehensive study carried on by experts in their respective fields lays the foundation for action. Only those communities that recognize the need for such planning are apt to get the funds and personnel necessary for implementation. Smaller communities, however, that have the foresight and will to rehabilitate may also make a beginning and perhaps even succeed.

The Beginning in Independence

The Zionic Research Institute has carried on similar, though not as extensive, studies in Independence with excellent participation and helpful results. The committee consisted of executive personnel from the City of Independence Department of Health, the Independence Sanitarium and Hospital, the Human Resources Corporation, and Social Ministries of the church.

Research has been done in the areas of service, creative community planning, and analytical study of existing communities (areas referred to by Breckenfield as "urban sociology").

I can touch but briefly on the many facets of the broad program of the Restoration church to "seek to bring forth and establish the cause of Zion." I have emphasized that those revelations dealing with this commission not only delineate a program of community building but establish the principles upon which men are to govern their social, economic, and spiritual lives. Personal and group stewardships, the exercise of free agency, the storehouse as basis of the distribution of resources and wealth, the gathering of those of kindred minds and spirits, the function of the Aaronic priesthood as an extension of the arm of the Bishopric in assisting the lonely and poor and distressed all center in the life and ministry of Jesus Christ who gave to men the gift of the Comforter. The ultimate purpose is that men may be blessed both in this life and in eternity. For this purpose we are "in the world...."

One of the finest programs for community involvement, functioning in Independence, is that of neighborhood councils. The origin of this program is given in the report of the Subcommittee on Citizen Involvement as follows:

The Subcommittee on Citizen Involvement was established as an agency of the Citizens Goals Committee in response to a challenge given by Mayor Phil K. Weeks as reported in the *Examiner* for January 2, 1971:

"We need a greater involvement of people in the affairs of the city. I feel that the Goals Committee can be the nucleus of a city-wide cooperative effort to make this a better place to live."

An amplified description of the purpose of the committee appeared in the *Independence Observer* of January 14: "... city officials are vitally interested in seeing that more and more citizens have a voice in what happens in the city. The city council is anxious to find new ways of determining the opinions and feelings of local citizens before making major decisions in their council sessions.

"... the mayor felt that while the citizen involvement represented in the Citizens Goals Committee was good, additional ways should be sought to expand such citizen participation."

Background

The foundation for the work of the subcommittee actually began when this nation began and is caught up in the phrase which describes the American dream: government "of the people, by the people, and for the people." A look at today's society, however, does not speak well for the fulfillment of the dream.

Everywhere cities are in trouble. The problems of minorities have not been solved. Bond proposals, designed by school officials to improve education for the children of our cities, fail apparently because the voters are unconvinced of the need or are unwilling to pay the cost. A general disenchantment with government at all levels seems to characterize the mood of the people right at a time when the problems are so immense that the need for wise government is greater than it has ever been.

... George Romney, speaking from his perspective as the federal official responsible for urban development, has identified the problem in this way: "We have no model of what a city should be like."

The subcommittee has accepted this fact as an additional challenge as we have sought to find a method by which the city of Independence could become a model for other cities—a model of citizen participation in civic affairs "to make this a better place to live."

I quote further from the report:

The Plan

The essential elements of the plan for increased citizen involvement, as revised, are the organization of

(1) *Neighborhood Councils* in every neighborhood; the organization of a
(2) *Citizens Advisory Council* composed of the presidents of Neighborhood Councils; the organization of
(3) *Citizens Committees* for every department in the city; and the organization of
(4) *Citizens Workshops and Assemblies* for monthly communication sessions.

This project may well be one of the finest efforts toward community development ever undertaken in this area.

Pilot Community Project

On August 30, 1969, a seminar on the pilot community was held at the Stone Church Education Building. The two years preceding that, preliminary plans for the development of such a community were formulated. Out of this steps were taken to form the Rainbow Development Corporation and the Harvest Hills Association.

This project may prove helpful in paving the way for further developments pertaining to the gathering and community building.

Considerable study and careful planning have been given the project by those who are sponsoring it. As is always the case with communities having special social and religious objectives, there have been problems. Growth has not been rapid; however at the time of this writing (1973) land has been purchased, the first housing unit constructed, and the second begun.

Excerpts from the preface and introduction of a brochure on the project sets forth these purposes for the proposed community:

Two corporations, with overlapping board membership, are involved in the proposed development of a new community of approximately 1,000 acres of land located in the east Independence suburb: Rainbow Development Corporation is a for-profit organization under the Missouri statutes, which will assemble the land and undertake the construction as designated by the Harvest Hills Association. The latter organization is incorporated as a not-for-profit corporation under the statutes of Missouri. Anyone may become an investor in the former. Only residents of the community will be members of the latter cooperative association.

The basic purpose and objective of this new experimental community is to create a wholesome living environment wherein the values it represents are "spiritual as well as physical, aesthetic as well as monetary, beautiful as well as healthy, spacious as well as clean, well balanced as well as carefully patrolled." This will involve not only the best physical planning concepts, but also social, economic, and cultural activities which would be conducive to neighborliness and a community esprit de corps which would result in a high degree of citizen participation and involvement in the issues of the day.

Although the motivation for initiating such a community experiment stems primarily from a group of members of the Reorganized

247

Church of Jesus Christ of Latter Day Saints in Independence, Missouri, there is no intent that participation be limited along any religious denominational lines, but rather, any and all who share the common bond of peace and brotherhood throughout the world will be welcome regardless of race, creed, color, or national origin. Hopefully it might become known as an international settlement in the true American tradition as a "melting pot" of peoples from all nations.

... A major socioeconomic objective will be to create a community "surplus" through voluntary contributions of time, talent, and resources and various self-help projects which will enable a minimum desirable standard of living (food, clothing, shelter, medical care, education, employment, recreation, cultural pursuits) without any compulsion or social pressure for conspicuous consumption or "Keeping up with the Joneses."

Anyone considering joining this or a similar project should take time to meet with those sponsoring it, then make his own evaluation. Success in any such community endeavor depends upon the individuals participating in it—their financial ability; their willingness to assume a share of the work, money, time, and effort; and their cooperation. Communities do not grow and become stable without good planning. Neither can there be a successful community unless there are people who are willing to make the initial effort.

FAITH FOR THE FUTURE

As I review that which I have written I realize that I have covered many subjects and expressed many thoughts intended to show the place of the Restoration church in a world of change from its inception to the present. I have tried to state my deep convictions of faith in the future of our church and our society. I have always felt that isolation is neither possible nor desirable. Service to the community is both a privilege and a responsibility. It need never be a tedious or uninteresting experience, though it well may be time-consuming and tiring. The rewards which come from working with people of different faiths, political philosophies, and national or racial backgrounds are ample payment for such investments.

I have not attempted to list the many community projects in which it has been my privilege to participate. I have come to know many concerned citizens serving in this metropolitan area. From such volunteers who have contributed so much to the meeting of human needs I have received more by way of counsel, comradeship, inspiration, and challenge than I can ever repay. I silently thank them and all others with whom it has been my good fortune to be associated in public service.

Hopefully my love for the church is reflected in this

book. I bring it to a close with a note of deep appreciation for the three presidents with whom I have served, their counselors, the Council of Twelve, the Seventy, and many members of the priesthood.

In the Presiding Bishopric my counselors—Clarence A. Skinner, Henry L. Livingston, and Walter N. Johnson—served with distinction. Members of the Order of Bishops gave outstanding support in many projects in addition to their individual assignments. Above all, perhaps, I should thank the members of the church as a whole, for in the final analysis they have met the exigencies, trials, and costs of moving the church toward the kingdom.

I write this final note of thanks trusting that it may convey to others my deep faith in God and Jesus Christ, and praying that I may ever remember to search for the truth revealed in scripture as "the light which now shineth, which giveth you light, is through him who enlighteneth your eyes, which is the same light which quickeneth your understandings; which light proceedeth forth from the presence of God, to fill the immensity of space" (Doctrine and Covenants 85:3a).